MY LIFE MY *Story*

CLAIRVOYANT MEDIUM
AND SPIRITUAL HEALER

NOEL SORBIE

Copyright © 2021 by Noel Sorbie

All rights reserved. No part of this publication may be reproduced, distributed, or transmitted in any form or by any means, including photocopying, recording, or other electronic or mechanical methods, without the prior written permission of the publisher, except in the case of brief quotations embodied in critical reviews and certain other noncommercial uses permitted by copyright law.

Book Design by HMDpublishing

My Life
My Story

This book is dedicated to my mam and dad who brought me into the world and blessed me with infinite love and devotion, and who taught me how to appreciate the precious gift of life, whilst encouraging me to follow my dreams.

Contents

Introduction 8
The Early Years 11
Mischief & Mayhem 18
Animal Magic 22
A Damaged Soul 26
The Aliens Have Landed 31
Feeling Protected 36
Raging Hormones 40
Is There Anybody There? 45
Haunted House 49
The Camaraderie 53
The Perils Of Dutch Courage 55
Hot Stuff 60
A Satisfied Audience 63
Visit From An Angel 66
Spiritual Healing 70
Mixing With The Stars 76
Never Refuse A Pint 81
Journey To Ibiza 84
High-Society Friendships 90
To Find A Cure 94
Family Values 97
Convincing A Sceptic 99

Psychic Fairs	101
Letters, Extracts & Testimonies	104
Epilogue	108
Acknowledgements	113

Introduction

When I was three years old, I heard a man's voice; he spoke unexpectedly as though out of thin air. Yet he spoke as if he knew me, using my name as I tried to familiarise myself with him. I didn't think for one moment that this was strange as I'd already started to see people in my bedroom that I knew no one else could see. I'd been having what I can only describe as out-of-body experiences where people would visit me and take me to another land like they were whisking me off through time and space where I was never on my own. I would make friends with other children in these faraway lands and Mum would tell me it was all in my imagination – one of those imaginary friends that so many children experience. But are they really imaginary?

As children, we often choose experiences that we would shy away from as an adult because we've learnt, throughout life, that what we do can impact on others. We ask questions as children with a constant need to know why and a permanent curiosity that helps us to learn. And even though the answers we receive may not be quite what we expected to hear, it always gives us a better understanding of the world around us. Humans have an inner fear that could prevent them from accepting the truth: They choose to discard the uncomfortable feelings as they get older in favour of living a more carefree existence, a desire to live freely without the need to question. And, as children, we are given a choice to live a spiritual path where we are able to listen and learn to our higher-self or, perhaps, ignore it.

It is from an early age that we start our journey on the spiritual path, a journey that has already been chosen for us. Some children decide, subconsciously, not to acknowledge the spirit world and they go on to have a wonderful childhood, filled with love and serenity and happy thoughts, whilst others will discover a side to themselves that is able to connect with their higher-self and take them on a pathway that will lead them to understand about the wiser beings that surround us such as 'Guardian Angels' or 'Guides'. As we begin on this journey, one of these beings is assigned to us, leading the way to the next stage where we will enter a higher plane and be introduced to a new level on this spiritual path. As we enter each level, the guide that has taken us thus far will step back and allow another to take its place, and we also refer to these beings as 'Doorkeepers'. Can you imagine each one standing by the door as we approach, their featherlight hand resting on the handle as they get ready to open it and take over the role as our 'Guide'? Close your eyes for a moment and imagine how secure this will make you feel, knowing you don't have to begin a life-changing journey with no one by your side.

Your Angel is there to protect you. They see you make good and bad decisions, and even though they can only guide you along the way, they will always help to put you back on the track that was always there for you to tread. But as we get further along in our spiritual journey, we learn that as humans it *is* okay to make bad decisions, not because we have a higher being around that is watching out for us, but because by making those decisions it is helping us to learn how to make the good ones. It's like someone watching you as you choose to turn left when your journey is supposed to make you turn right; you will keep going until you realise it was the wrong way whilst your Angel or Guide steers you back to where you should be. Then, when you look back on the endless pathways that you took whilst growing up, the lefts that should have been rights and the rights that should have been lefts, the crossroads that beckoned decisions you felt too scared to take, you suddenly start to realise the pieces that fit together; the decisions you made, albeit perhaps not quite right in the long-run, were leading you to where you are today. That's what helps us grow and learn and realise where we went wrong in life, as well as where we went right.

The Early Years

It's difficult to know where to start telling you about my life because so far, it's been particularly eventful for many different reasons. So, I'm going to start at the beginning, because, as Julie Andrews sang many years ago, "We'll start at the very beginning. It's a very good place to start."

I was born on 3rd March 1950 to loving parents, Lilian and Frederick. Mum was beautiful and graceful and admired by many. She was a ballet teacher and thirty-eight years old when she gave birth to me. My dad, much older at sixty-two, was a retired watchmaker and jeweller and both my parents were my role models from a very young age. One of my earliest childhood memories was when Mum jokingly said, "That lad doesn't know the meaning of the word 'no'" and I replied with a cheeky grin, "What does 'no' mean, Dad?"

Born in a large family in 1888, Dad had two brothers and four sisters and lived in the West End of Newcastle in a town called Elswick. His mum was a housewife, though with seven children and a hardworking husband to look after, her days were filled to capacity with chores and seeing to her loved ones, something most women back in those days tended to do as second nature whilst their husbands went out to work. They, like most others in the town, lived in poverty as welfare wasn't around back then and unless the work was available, it meant they simply went without. Something they never went without however, was love, and that was taught to Dad and his siblings throughout their childhood. The children didn't always have shoes and would often be known to run from Newcastle to Whitley Bay to do whatever errands were needed in return for a mere shilling. It was simply a case of, if you didn't work back then, you starved.

From a very young age, Dad developed a fascination with clocks and quickly learned how to fix them, along with fob watches that were all the rage in the early 1900s. By the age of nineteen, he had successfully built up his own business and had customers needing his expertise from all around the Northeast of England. But in 1915, when he was still a young man at the age of twenty-eight, the business folded and he lost everything. It was a particularly difficult time for him due to having built up a large clientele. Dad, not shy of hard work and needing to make a living, began working for his brother, Alex, and stayed there for seven years. With a sense of pride and a determination to be successful again, Dad eventually managed to save up enough money to set up his business once more.

By the time he was thirty-five, along with his renewed business opportunity, he joined the Royal Flying Corps and became a co-pilot. This was a time in his life when he met some very famous people, a few of these being Wyatt Earp, Wild Bill Hickok, and Annie Oakley. As a young boy, I would listen intently to the stories he told about his connections to these legendary celebrities, my eyes wide as he recalled conversations whilst mimicking their accents like a pro.

My mum, on the other hand, born in 1911 to a family with the double-barrel surname of Horsfall-Bowes, had, perhaps you could say, a more refined upbringing by her father who worked for the welfare, and was also a stage director who organised professional dance shows, some of which Mum performed in. She would go on to dance on stage for several years along with the troupe my grandfather had created, until one day she fell in love and married her first husband, James, with whom she had a daughter, my half-sister, Anne. Following in Mum's footsteps as a dancer, Anne also became a brilliant ice-skater, which made our mum incredibly proud. At an unfortunately young age, Mum's first husband passed away after contracting Tuberculosis, which naturally devastated the family and left my mum and Anne heartbroken.

But not one to stay down for long and a woman who insisted on getting on with her life no matter what, she eventually accepted James' untimely demise and went on to meet my dad. It was, after everything Mum had been through, love at first sight for the two of them as their eyes met one night at a dog-racing track; maybe not the most romantic place to meet, but nonetheless, it was the place they would begin their lives together and raise their family.

When I was born in 1950, my maternal grandmother, a retired opera singer who had decided to spend her time supporting my grandfather, used to accommodate people with theatrical backgrounds in her home and I will always remember being there one day and hearing the calming, dulcet tones of the famous actor, Howard Keel as he belted out *'Oh, What a Beautiful Morning...'* It's always been one of those songs that gets stuck in my head and brings back the particularly poignant memory of when he sat me on his knee as though he was just some ordinary paying guest singing to an audience who wished to listen.

Treading the boards ran in the family, though perhaps stopped with me when Mum tried in vain to get me up on stage after teaching me to tap dance. I refused every time; dancing on stage just wasn't going to be my thing however much I admired Mum for doing it so expertly. Even though her attempts to teach me fell flat, she was a huge success at teaching others, especially people with disabilities, both physical and hidden. Something she was exceptionally good at was teaching deaf people how to communicate by using dance moves from the vibrations through the floor. Audiences would watch the performances, fascinated and in awe at Mum's talent as many of her students expressed themselves with laughter and happy faces, thrilled to be able to take part in something they would most likely never have got the chance to do. Seeing this for myself always made me feel so proud of my parents and what they'd achieved, not to mention the loving upbringing they'd given me. It goes without saying that I was a fortunate child, lucky to have been raised by two beautiful human beings.

When Dad's business in the West End was once again established, our family lived above the shop in which he sold jewellery, including uncut diamonds and watches, along with a selection of rather opulent Grandfather clocks. Mum would often leave me in my pram outside in the back lane behind the shop, while she did her daily chores and Dad tended to his customers and carried out repairs. Despite being so young at only nine months old, I can recall a ginger Tom cat that would lay across the pram, perhaps for warmth and comfort. After this happened a few times, I managed to undo the bib-flap that Mum had fastened to protect me from the rain, and the cat snuggled itself inside the pram and lay against me. Keeping both of us warm, it obviously decided my pram would become its new bed and I guess it acted as my own substitute teddy bear back in those early days.

But one day, snuggled and warm as it lay with me, a young couple were walking past and approached me in the pram, poking their heads in to say hello and no doubt coo at the baby they maybe would have liked for themselves. As the man reached in to lift me out, the cat leapt from nowhere and latched its claws onto his throat, scratching and hissing as he tried to fend it off, before jumping back in complete shock. The cat continued to hold its grip at which point my mum ran outside upon hearing the cat's ear-piercing howls and the poor man's screams. Mum, always protective, decided the couple looked dodgy and threatened to call the police if they didn't leave. Taking the cat from around the man's neck, scratches prominent as he rubbed the bleeding wounds it had caused, they finally retreated and left Mum and me in peace. Quite shaken, Mum put the cat on the floor and it casually sauntered away, as cats tend to do quite well. And for the next three years, Mum fed that cat whenever it came back to visit. Even though it was always somewhat feral and not in the least bit a domestic feline, our bond continued as it carried on making itself warm and comfortable on my lap.

One cloudy day whilst at the front of the shop, the ginger Tom cat looked up at me, stared straight into my eyes, then turned around and walked directly in front of an oncoming car. It was killed on impact. At almost four years old, I knew, even then, that my beloved companion was telling me, "I've done my job of protecting you and now my time is up." My heart was broken that day. It took me a good six months to come to terms with losing my friend, but I guess I also realised that the cat had come into my life for a reason as it was then that I discovered there was something within me that was different to others, where I would talk to people that no other living person could see. This was the start of my spiritual development and a time in my life that was probably the most significant.

I could often hear people talking to me, yet no one was anywhere to be seen. Voices, laughter, people trying to communicate with me. And whilst it may seem strange to some, it felt almost calming to me. One incident happened when I felt like I was in a classroom, when I was, in fact, in Dad's shop. I suppose at the time I was bored, a young boy needing to find something to play with, not mature enough to know there were no toys in a jewellery shop! Being quite adventurous, I climbed onto the table and looked around the room. Tools and repair equipment had been neatly stored away on shelves, as items of jewellery and leather-strap watches sat upon fabric cushions. That was when I spotted something sparkling, an array of precious stones meticulously arranged and looking, to a young boy, like something worth exploring. I took the stones off the shelf and began to play with them as though they were marbles, throwing each one into the air and challenging myself to catch them again. When I decided to throw them all at the same time however, I didn't realise they would scatter through the air and roll all over the floor, causing me to shout out, "Oh, no!"

Upon hearing my cry for help, Dad rushed into the shop assuming I'd fallen off a chair, before seeing me kneeling on the floor in desperation to find my new toys. "Those twinkly stones have gone through the floorboards," I said to my very shocked father who for a moment couldn't speak. "Lilian!" he shouted, "come and look what this boy has done now. He's thrown my diamonds all over the shop." I think that might be the first recollection of me seeing Dad angry. It didn't happen often, which is why that moment always sticks in my mind.

For the next few days, him and my brothers spent their time on hands and knees with magnifying glasses, searching for each stone. I never did hear the last of that story!

Mischief & Mayhem

As Dad got older, he retired and sold the shop and moved our family to Benwell, another town in the West End of Newcastle. I made new friends there and was a typical young boy, getting up to all sorts and trying to stay out of trouble, yet often failing miserably. I remember an orchard in the area filled with apple trees; large, green, juicy-looking fruit that we, as youngsters, were determined to get at. Unfortunately, a high wall hindered us from picking the apples and we tried many ways to get over it. After a bit of problem solving and some daredevil tactics, we eventually managed to scale that wall and found ourselves in the rather plush gardens of a big house. Our eyes were fixed on the apples as they temptingly dangled from every branch, ripe for picking. Each one of us took a few, munching on one as we stuffed others into pockets. But, to our horror, the owner of the house came out and not knowing what to do, we all scarpered in opposite directions, unsure which way to make our escape. I, along with another boy, were caught by the man as he grabbed our jackets and held us at arm's length. Nodding towards the door of the house, he said, "Next time you want to get into the orchard, just knock on the door and I'll let you in." We never went back after that. "Where's the fun in being allowed to just walk straight in rather than scale a high wall and have the thrill of knowing you're doing something you shouldn't be doing?" one boy said, and the rest of us agreed wholeheartedly.

I was a rebellious youngster and needed a lot of attention to stop me getting bored. Being Mum and Dad to me was a full-time job for my parents and they would often take me to my nana's house in Sunderland - my mum's mum. There, I would occasionally meet up with my cousin, Irena, whose dad, Alfonce, was Polish and fought in World War Two. Being interested in the war, I would sit for hours listening to him telling me stories about events that took place, the horrors and atrocities that the war was littered with. I'll always remember one such story Alfonce told: When he was in the Resistance, one day he was driving a truck that he had assumed was filled with German soldiers in the back. When he heard one speak Polish, he stopped the truck and got out, then walked round to the back and opened the door. "Who spoke Polish?" he asked the sea of surprised faces as they looked at him like a collection of guppy fish. Each one spoke at the same time. "We all do," they said, much to his surprise. It turned out they were actually young men dressed in German uniforms on their way to the front line. Alfonce said, "It's your lucky day because I was going to drive this truck off the cliff." And with that, he let them all get out before telling them to go home.

Another time, Alfonce was running towards the border where he picked up three children. Unfortunately, he couldn't keep hold of all three and one fell from his grasp, but he managed to get the other two over the border whilst German soldiers continuously fired shots at them. I always used to think how exciting his life sounded, yet horrific at the same time.

Married to my mum's sister, Betty, they had three children of their own, all quite tough. One day, I was playing with my next-door neighbour's son, Richard, when two grown up lads took it upon themselves to start bullying me. As brave and carefree as I was, I didn't particularly want to square up to these two at the time and told Irena about what was going on. She waited for them and laid into them, bashing them up and threatening them, and they never came near my nana's house ever again!

Even though times were still quite hard back in those days, my parents used to take me on holidays to the seaside and always ensured I never needed or wanted for anything. I guess you could say I was spoilt, perhaps being the youngest, but Dad being retired meant he could spend more time with me than if he'd still been running the business.

On one of these holidays, we went to the circus – I was about six years old and was accompanied by my sister, Anne, and her husband, Ronnie Peart. At fourteen years older, she was deemed responsible to take care of me and would sometimes look after me, probably to give my parents a break! I remember this particular day vividly when we were at the circus, and I saw a lion in a cage. Deciding I wanted to talk to it, I approached its enclosure and took in its beautiful coat, admiring its magnificence as it stood proudly, perhaps a little perturbed at the intentions of a young boy with mischief in his eyes. I had a sudden urge to squeeze myself in between the bars of the cage and just managed to get my head through, before beginning to manoeuvre my body inside. My overwhelming feeling to stroke the lion made me reach out my arm and touch its fur, gently easing my fingers through the soft strands. I had no fear at all, and it didn't cross my mind that this animal could be potentially dangerous. But because of my lack of fear, the lion didn't feel threatened and allowed me to continue stroking it, before casually starting to lick me as though this was a perfectly normal thing for any wild creature to do.

When Anne and Ronnie saw me sitting in the cage with the lion seemingly at ease with the bond we had created, they rushed towards me, frantic with worry, reaching through the bars to pull me out. When they stood me up outside the cage, the lion still nonchalant to its space being invaded by a six-year-old boy, they grabbed my hand and wouldn't let go for the rest of the time we were at the circus. Suffice to say, I got a good telling off when I got back home that day!

Animal Magic

Anne and Ronnie worked on Ronnie's family farm, and it was somewhere I went to visit occasionally, usually in the hope that I'd stay out of trouble. There was one instance when I jumped into a hole, and unbeknownst to me, it was a sewage pit! Not knowing how deep it was until I'd landed in it, I thought I was going to drown and shouted for help, only to be found and hauled out completely covered in sewage. The stench was so bad that I had to be scrubbed down with the end of a yard brush and ice-cold water. You can imagine if I'd have had a tail, it would have been well and truly between my legs that day, not only with the freezing cold but with the shame of the whole experience. But I did like being on the farm because I've always had an affinity with animals. I would hear them talking to me as though putting thoughts in my head and on one occasion I could have sworn I heard a voice telling me, "*Open the barn door and let me out.*" As I did so, a flurry of excitement scurried past me in the form of furry black and white Border Collies, eager to escape their confinement and no doubt ready to start rounding up the sheep or, perhaps, make a bid for freedom. I tried telling Ronnie that the dogs had told me to open the barn door, but his expression told me he wasn't going to believe that and that, of course, led to yet another good telling off.

My connection with the animal kingdom has always been important to me. Walking on the fells one day I heard voices as though two people were talking nearby, yet no one was about for miles. On closer inspection as the voices continued, I spotted two hares a few feet away from me and they both lifted their silky heads in my direction, looked at me with startled expressions, then shot off at a significant speed. My heart goes out to the animals in our midst when I think how so many people fail to understand that they have a soul. They put their faith and trust in us, and many of these creatures rely on us to keep them safe, warm and fed, whilst fearing capture or abandonment, or cruelty for just being unable to communicate in a human voice.

In those early days as my spiritual journey began, I enjoyed sitting in the garden having childish conversations with the birds and rodents and they would talk back to me in an intellect only I could understand. One time I was sat on a stool and a blackbird appeared before me, its wing seemingly broken. I reached out my arm and took it into the palm of my hand, stroking its wing gently as its eyes focused on mine and a look of calmness overwhelmed its tiny features. Within a few minutes, it started to move freely before flying from my hand, its wing perhaps no longer in pain. It flew around the garden for a short time before coming back to me and hovering in front of my face as though to say, "*Thank you.*" I could physically feel its emotions penetrating my soul as it was obviously cured and once again free in its vast infinity. I also feel it with mice, rats, dogs, cats, foxes, even bees and insects. All living creatures have a soul and to me, it is a privilege to be at one with their thoughts.

At one house we lived in, the next-door neighbour had a cat and as we all know, cats tend to attack birds. One time in particular the cat did just this as I was playing outside, and the neighbour took it away and went to put it in the bin. But the bird was still alive, albeit injured from the attack. My initial instinct was fury at the neighbour's actions and I screamed at her, pulling at her dress and kicking out at her whilst shouting about how cruel I thought she was to do such a thing. Upon hearing my temper erupt, my parents came running outside to see what the fuss was about, asking their neighbour what was going on. Angry and shocked at my outburst, she said, "You need to keep your child under control," and I screamed back at her before turning to my mum and shouting in between sobs, "The lady put a bird in the bin and it's still alive."

Mum went to the bin and lifted the lid, only to see the small, terrified creature lying on top of the rubbish that was already in there. My joy at rescuing the injured bird was soon overshadowed when Mum discovered another bird inside the bin that had already been killed. It broke my heart that day to think people were so cruel. My view on life is that every form has a right to live and no creature deserves to be killed needlessly, either for sport or otherwise, especially if it can be saved.

My fascination around the nature spirits was always something I treasured as I'd play in the garden communicating with butterflies that would flutter around me and the bees that seemed to hover. One summer's day whilst playing on my own in the back garden, I was quite sure that I heard a voice call my name and it made me stop what I was doing as I looked around me. Amongst the nature spirits that were keeping me company, I witnessed a beautiful array of lights all the colours of the rainbow, jumping about as though dancing before my eyes. I was still a young boy and even though I could hear voices whispering and saying things to me that sounded clear enough to interpret, I didn't understand quite what they were trying to tell me as they kept saying I would experience amazing things happening all over the world. I suppose, as a child, it was magical to see these images before me, but I didn't know what being an adult would bring as I continued my communication with the colourful creatures that adorned my garden.

A Damaged Soul

At the age of six, I got friendly with Billy, the boy who lived next door to us. He was a nice enough young lad and a little older than me. I felt proud to call him my friend and we would chat together and talk about school and animals and things young boys got up to in the 1950s. Perhaps I looked up to him in a way, being friends with someone older than me that took an interest in my wellbeing and wanted to spend time with me.

But then, one day, Billy sexually assaulted me.

I didn't understand what was happening, or why, but I knew it wasn't right because each time he did it, he would threaten me if I were ever to tell anyone. These events, quite understandably, gave me nightmares and made me withdraw from normal childhood, leaving my parents questioning why I'd suddenly gone from the mischievous little scallywag to a shy child who didn't want to join in anymore and wasn't interested in the childish antics a six-year-old boy would normally engage in. Unsure how to broach the subject, knowing I needed to due to the fact I knew something was wrong with my friendship with Billy, I finally plucked up the courage to break the news to Dad about what was going on, and because of how I described what Billy was doing, Dad knew I was telling the truth.

Naturally, he was incandescent with rage, as any loving parent would be to hear their child was being sexually abused. His first port of call after my announcement was to speak to Billy's parents, a conversation, to this day, I know little about, mainly because I managed to block the abuse out of my mind. I think, looking back, this was the start of my psychological issues as I kept this experience to myself, retreating into my shell and not wanting to join in anything at school. My teacher would shout at me because of my lack of wanting to learn and at the age of seven, after a mental break down, my mind was completely wiped clean and I was forced to start over, going back over the previous few years of education to learn from the beginning. I would go on to carry the burden of being abused for most of my adult life until in my sixties when I went through an extremely difficult phase and realised I needed to open up and talk about the feelings I'd harboured for all those years.

Because of having to start again, especially with my education, it became obvious that I had developed learning disabilities, which unfortunately made me the ideal target for bullies. I was eight years old by now, and still traumatised by what had happened to me, whilst kids in my class would laugh at me for being different. This, in turn, made me more frustrated at the world and I became angry and confused, unable to process rational thoughts or see people without being irritated by them. Even after what I had been through, I was still hearing voices and seeing souls that had passed on, and I never stopped believing I could heal animals with the emotional bond I had to them. That bond, however, didn't extend to humans back then as I didn't feel like I belonged anymore. I was convinced I'd been abducted by aliens and before long, my experiences with the world of spirit became more prominent as my mediumship, clairvoyance, and healing developed. I could hear people's thoughts and sense their feelings, but my anger was overwhelming as I would be unaware of things I said or did, often ostracizing myself from conversations and situations.

Once, when at my sister's house in Weardale, I believed there was someone in the house, an intruder coming up the stairs towards me. I darted towards a large wardrobe and moved it across the door in the hope it would stop whoever the mystery guest was coming in the room and finding me. I was eight years old at the time, just a small boy. My sister later told me that it would have taken three grown men to move that wardrobe and she simply couldn't understand how I'd managed it on my own. I truly believe unseen forces were in the room that day helping me shift that huge piece of heavy furniture, as I have always felt protected by something not of this world. Not long after that incident, my parents took me to see a psychologist who talked to me and concluded that I had an over-active mind and that I wasn't at all delusional. Whilst sat in that psychologist's office I told him, quite matter-of-factly, "Your brother, Harry, would like to tell you he is okay and he was sorry to leave you, that he didn't mean to do it, but it was a cry for help, and he was reaching out to his son." The psychologist was speechless. His dumbstruck expression prompted my dad to apologise. "I'm sorry my son came out with such nonsense," Dad said. But was soon put in his place when the psychologist replied, "Your son is exceptional. What he's just said to me makes perfect sense and I have no idea where he got it from." He went on: "There's nothing wrong with your son's mind; it's working perfectly normal. The only thing I can tell you is he is dyslexic." After that meeting, I was sent to a school for special educational needs, which in those days was given an unfortunate reputation as a school for 'backward' children.

Being so young meant I wasn't able, or experienced enough, to give much information to people, but I always recited what I knew or what I had been told.

Things improved with my mental health as time went on, mainly with the support of my parents, and when Dad was seventy years old, he got his dream job as a silver service waiter for the railways. Even though retired, he was always a worker and retirement didn't favour well in his world. Something he wasn't good at was handing over cash and I learnt at an early age that whenever he became tipsy, he was an easy target. Perhaps my mischievous streak was returning as one day when I saw him swaying down Normount Road near where we lived, I decided to try my luck. It was an opportunity not to be missed. "Hey, Dad," I said, contemplating whether I might need to hold him up as he stumbled towards me. "Could you let me have five pounds, please?" That was a lot of money back then and he didn't even ask me why I might want such a large amount. He simply fumbled about in his pocket and handed it over. "There you are, son," he said, handing it to me as I almost stumbled alongside him in shock. I couldn't believe I'd managed to get money out of him, let alone five pounds! The next day he told Mum that he thought he'd lost some money. "You probably spent it down the pub," she said, "or lost it in the street on your way back." To Dad, the whole incident was a complete mystery.

Not long after that day, I decided to come clean and admitted that I'd asked him for the money when he was drunk and that he'd most likely forgotten that he'd given it to me. I offered it back to him, but he said, "Keep it, son. Because you've been honest with me, you can have the five pounds, but make sure you save it. It's very important to save for your future." And with that, I hurried off before he could change his mind!

In those days I rarely listened to him. But looking back over the years, I knew he was right.

The Aliens Have Landed

As the years passed by, I spent more time at Anne and Ronnie's farm, which, at nearly three thousand acres, took some looking after. Around two thousand of those acres were fell, which is land for hill sheep where I would spend many days whiling away the time and communicating with the animals as though I was conversing with fellow humans.

In my early teens, a devastating sadness descended over our family when Anne and Ronnie lost their son to a chest infection at the age of two and a half. Darren was a sweet little boy and as you can imagine, it turned their world upside down and caused much heartbreak for the rest of us. Confused about why he had to die, I didn't fully understand what was going on and all sorts of thoughts raced through my head as I tried to work out why my nephew had been taken at such a young age.

I even believed back then that I had been abducted by aliens; I was convinced, in fact. I would shout out in my sleep, telling these 'aliens' to get away from me, yet for the years that followed they continued to visit, obviously not taking any notice of my pleas. It always seemed to be at night when they came to me. At first, I felt fearful, not understanding who or what they were, why they'd chosen *me*. But each time they arrived, they put calming thoughts in my head telling me not to be afraid, that they weren't going to hurt me but wanted to be my friend and wanted to study me. You may have heard stories of people who think they've been experimented on by aliens who've abducted them, and that's just how I felt. In my mind, I could see myself lying on a table with a blinding light above my head, shining into my eyes, similar to one you'd see in an operating theatre or at the dentist's. I'd have the sensation that a tube was being inserted into me and I'd then feel nauseous. Occasionally, I'd feel like I was floating in mid-air. I couldn't work out if they were communicating with me or each other and those feelings would increase with time as I continued trying to work out what they were saying. Yet, all the time these feelings of being overwhelmed by aliens took place, I got the strangest feeling also that my Guides were with me, protecting me from harm.

My head was all over the place and images in my mind showed people that I knew, living in an alternative dimension. It was like a parallel universe; the same as earth but everything the wrong way round. I felt that I was invincible, that I had special powers and could make things move, and this was something I was able to demonstrate many times. I believed I could move clouds and make it rain or make the sun shine down on us and light up the fields. My uncle would often comment that the fields needed rain and I would look up at the glorious blue sky, without a cloud in sight, and meditate. Occasionally, the rains would come, sometimes pounding against the earth as though the nature spirits had listened to my thoughts and answered my uncle's pleas for his crops to be watered. The spirits told me they didn't like humans upsetting the energy of the earth plane, and that humans only think about themselves, failing to understand there are other life forms still to be discovered. I believe they taught me that these life forms have more right to our planet than we humans do, and this made me feel truly connected to them.

Other countries and cultures believe strongly in these spirits and in Iceland, the government perform a ritual by asking them for permission to install a new pathway or road out of respect for the planet. You may think this all sounds farfetched, but I can assure you that I have had these experiences and have lived with them for most of my life. As humans still residing on our earth plane, we are merely custodians to keep our planet preserved, and it is simply showing respect for the place we call 'home'.

I remember one day back in 1963, when I was thirteen, I was, as usual, on Anne and Ronnie's family farm when it had snowed so heavily, the drifts prevented us from being able to see the house. I was helping to herd the sheep to safety by moving them into the sheds. So many were dying because of infection and cold and witnessing the exhaustion on both Ronnie and Uncle Tommy's faces through having to work twenty-four hours - and sometimes thirty-six hours non-stop - was a sight I will never forget. They had no choice but to keep the animals fed and watered, having to keep going out onto the fells to look for sheep that had been buried alive amidst the snow drifts. Anne would be doing her bit by making hot meals whenever one of them returned. The house was so cold that ice had formed on the insides of the windows and even with the fire spitting away and burning bright orange flames in the grate, it was impossible to keep warm.

However cold that house got, though, it fascinated me because I knew it was full of spirit activity. I would often hear muffled voices and unfamiliar noises when I lay in bed trying in vain to get warm, and one night, I recall a presence that I became aware of that felt somewhat threatening, creating a heavy atmosphere of oppression hanging in the room. I pulled the bedclothes over me, almost hiding from something I didn't quite understand, before sensing something standing over me at the side of the bed. It pressed down on the sheets as I continued to lie still. I wasn't scared; just curious.

This went on each night for a couple of weeks while I stayed at the farm, appearing at the same time, until one night, a little before its usual time, I decided to sit up in the bed and find out what, or who, was disturbing me. I looked towards the bedroom door and waited patiently. Within what felt like less than a minute, a shape wandered through the door and made its way to my bed, gliding along as though its legs didn't work. Even though I could make out it was a figure, it didn't look human and when it finally stood close to the side of my bed, I heard it make a grunting sound before emitting a heavy breathing noise as it moved right up to my face. I stayed calm. I didn't feel unsafe, and it had never attacked me on its previous visits, so I was sure it wouldn't do now. "What do you want?" I asked, but it didn't respond. As it finally left the room, I continued to show no fear, just a fascination for what was trying to make contact with me.

One of the most fascinating areas of the house for me was the attic, where I would spend copious amounts of time listening to strange noises after the latch would mysteriously open, as though inviting me to communicate. I bunked off school once or twice to sit in the attic, assuming no one would find me up there. But one day, I did get caught when someone found me after venturing up there to get something, obviously shocked to see me sat, in what to them would have looked like a room in the eaves used as a general dumping ground. Of course, I should have been in school, not hiding out amongst a pile of old suitcases and several boxes of unwanted items! For misbehaving like that back then, you'd get a good scolding by both the teachers *and* your parents, would probably have to go to bed early for nights on end and not be able to use the school tuck shop. We didn't get grounded in those days, but neither were we let off lightly with a few words of advice and a 'don't do it again' from the headmaster. I'd always struggled with school, especially since my breakdown, and would go into rages mostly out of frustration and being socially inept. My communication skills weren't great with my peers *or* the staff, though I always managed to communicate fine with the spirit world who visited me regularly and enabled me to see people that had passed over; people that others on the earth plane couldn't see. It was difficult for me on the whole as I still didn't truly understand my mission in life was to be a channel between the spirit and earth planes, and the spirits, perhaps looking back in hindsight, were putting me through hell as they would relentlessly try and make me understand what I had to do. It was a calling that would gift me with friends and associates throughout my life and take me to many different places in order to reach out and bring comfort to those in need.

Feeling Protected

Life as a young boy was a constant adventure and looking back, as I often do, the things we got up to could be seen today as dangerous, as well as completely off-limits. It wasn't unusual for us to play in derelict buildings, some that just about hung on for dear life until a gust of wind might tear it down, and there we were, carefree and thinking we were invincible, having a great time. Of course, when I do look back on those frivolous days of being a tearaway, I cringe and wonder how on earth I got away with not being seriously hurt, or even killed, as could quite easily have happened in some of the places we explored.

One such memory takes me back to an old warehouse we'd decided to play in, completely unsafe and one that perhaps should have been demolished. Today, I suspect an electric fence would surround it along with signs about the dangers of being anywhere near. But back then, kids took that chance themselves; being told where you could and couldn't play just wasn't an issue and even though my parents would likely have gone ballistic should they have known where I hung out, my rebellious streak always took precedence over the sensible approach! So, there I was, exploring the top floor of this extremely rackety old building with worm-infested floorboards and water dripping from just about everywhere conceivable, when, all of a sudden, I heard a voice: "Don't step forward." For a second or two I thought it was one of my friends having seen something that I hadn't and probably warning me. But what I'd actually heard was a grown man's voice, a gruff instruction that stopped me in my tracks. I sheepishly looked around, feeling very strongly that this man, whom I couldn't physically see, was watching me and wanting to communicate. I remember thinking it was probably him that had made the floorboards creak, a distinctive noise trying to alert me to his presence.

I eventually made my way back down to the ground floor where my friends were waiting, not quite brave enough to have ventured to the top with me. "You look pale," one of them pointed out when I approached them, "you look like you've seen a ghost!" I asked if they'd seen anyone else in the building, a man wandering about perhaps, knowing deep down that they hadn't. I went on to tell them he'd spoken to me, that I clearly heard his voice telling me not to step forward. Their shocked faces told me they believed I hadn't made it up and as their imaginations starting to run away with them and the ghost stories began, almost scaring each other to death with 'what' could be in this derelict warehouse with us, we heard another noise. It was an old, discarded vacuum cleaner having mysteriously been switched on in an adjacent empty room where one of my friends had been exploring. He came charging out of the room, white as a sheet, announcing that the vacuum had started to glide around the floor as though being pushed by someone. This particular friend wasn't one to make up stories and just seeing the shock on his face was enough proof to know he hadn't switched it on himself. I knew there was a spirit in the building that day, trying to communicate with us. When, whoever it was started to cough once the noise of the vacuum cleaner stopped, I decided to take that spirit seriously and gave him a name: John.

Each of our visits to that warehouse over the next few months resulted in John being there with us. His presence became the norm as we'd continue playing there and he would continue watching us, probably keeping us safe. Of course, back then we didn't have mobile phones or computer games and so our days off school were spent doing stuff you'd never get away with these days, for example, setting off bangers inside, something you'd probably get arrested for in this day and age, even if you were caught with one in your possession. We never came to any significant harm, though we always went home with the odd scraped knee and cuts and bruises that our parents would tut at, shake their heads, then be satisfied that we'd managed to stay out of trouble.

There was a forest near our house where we'd play 'Pirates' by the little stream that ran through it. We connected a thick piece of rope from a tree at one side of the stream to a tree at the other side and would swing on it, pretending we were Tarzan whilst mimicking, *"Ah, ah, ah, ah, ahhhh,"* - that iconic sound that he made. It was great fun, if not a bit scary at times, especially when I didn't quite make the other side on one occasion and fell, what felt like to a young boy, a long way down onto the rocks that lay on the bed of the stream. A bit woeful at being somewhat battered and bruised, I managed to get out and climb the bank back to safety. No harm done as such, though my pride had taken a bit of a bashing! But the fact was, I always felt as though something, or someone, was watching out for me, making sure I never came to any harm apart from the perils of being a boy filled with hopeful, opportunistic tendencies for adventure.

One day, however, I had an unfortunate collision with a car that I didn't notice was hurtling towards me. It was a miracle I wasn't hurt and looking back at that incident, I realise how extremely lucky I was. The car suffered a small dent where it had crashed into me, but once again, I felt as though my life was being spared by an unseen force. After that, I started to wonder whether I had super-powers and could maybe even fly, and one day I fell from the top floor of a disused building and landed on the ground unscathed. As I fell, my body seemed to float through the air, weightlessly, and I know I could have easily broken several bones that day.

Raging Hormones

As teenagers we tend to develop a rebellious streak, and I was no exception. I wasn't a bad lad, but just enjoyed the frivolity of being young and carefree, and of course, growing into a man. I wanted the muscles and fitness and the girls to like me, just like most boys my age, and at fifteen, I enjoyed a good friendship with a few lads from my area. Along with two mates called Ray-one and Ray-two - given nicknames to stop the confusion - one called John, and another called Billy, we had some fun times, hanging around the streets, doing a bit of this, bit of that, and were generally a bunch of happy-go-lucky teens who just craved adventure. We dreamed of becoming footballers but none of us were fit enough to make the cut and so between us, we hired a fitness instructor who unfortunately put us through hell with his fitness regime. There we were, in all weathers, training three times a week like we were on a mission to be the next Bobby Charlton, building up muscle strength and stamina and hoping that one day we'd be on that pitch with the other greats.

It was during the summer of 1965 when Ray-one's dad asked us all if we'd like to go to their caravan on holiday. It was a decent sized caravan parked on Crimdon Dene Holiday Park in Hartlepool, so not too far away to travel. Money was tight back then and as a group of teenagers, we didn't have much spare cash apart from the bit of spending money we'd managed to save. But nonetheless, off we went, arriving at the caravan one evening when the sun was just going down. Our first job, being horny teenage lads was, of course, to check out the girls on the site. After all, it wouldn't have been much fun if we couldn't have at least hooked up with some of them and shown off the stamina we'd started to develop since the fitness training was starting to pay off.

You probably remember the days when you could get fish and chips in newspaper? Well, that's what we did on that first night, made our way to the nearest fish and chip shop - chippy for short - where we congregated outside and didn't speak for fifteen minutes whilst we guzzled down our fish supper, newspaper print all over our fingers and the chip fat oil running down our chins. I can still taste those fish suppers all these years later!

Our next stop was the local pub. Now, even though we were still only fifteen, I looked a lot older for my years and it was therefore always me who had to pretend to be old enough to go in pubs and shops and buy the stuff we were under the legal age to buy. Things weren't quite so strict in those days however, and I suppose retailers were mainly glad of the custom, though it didn't always make it easier for me as a young lad who was still relatively naïve. Something I was always expected to buy was condoms and nine times out of ten, you could guarantee I'd go into the shop to come face-to-face with an attractive female assistant behind the counter. That used to put me right off! I'd end up leaving the shop with umpteen packets of chewing gum and a new comb, but that was me, embarrassed at the thought of buying something with the intention of having sex, from a woman who was much older and wiser than me and probably dying to laugh at my determined courage.

Halfway through the week away in that caravan, having a great time just on our own, making our mark on the site and letting everyone know that we'd landed, Ray-one and I came across a couple of really nice girls called Anne and Lynn. Good looking and with slim figures, we became quite smitten with them and after plucking up the courage to ask them out, we were thrilled when they agreed to meet us on the beach that night. Off we went to the local chemist where I had the deed of facing another female assistant behind the counter, plucking up the courage to buy a packet of condoms, before we then made our way to meet our two new companions, horny as hell and hoping for the best.

The girls, much to our delight, turned up, and we got chatting whilst sat on the sand, talking about all sorts from football to fitness to holidays in caravans and what we got up to at home. What was great about meeting people back then was that we didn't have mobile phones and weren't distracted by scrolling Facebook and checking emails. We talked, laughed, and communicated with each other. We looked at each other properly, face to face, not just on a profile picture whilst discussing politics with someone you'd never meet. It was so much more personal, but that made it easier, too, because you could see expressions on the faces of the people you talked to, and I liked that. You noticed eyes light up and smiles appear; hand gestures and those little tell-tale signs that someone liked you. It all seemed honest and open, somehow.

As the night wore on and the conversation flowed, it became clear the girls were up for some fun with us and suffice to say, the condoms got used, albeit with trepidation as they were pretty rubbish quality back in those days. We went back to our respective caravans at the end of the night, satisfied and feeling rather content at scoring perhaps more than we thought we would, and had a damn good night's sleep! The following day, being the horny devils that we were, we met up with another two girls from the site and ended up two-timing Anne and Lynn. We were kids, enjoying the freedom of youth and revelling in being the charmers that we were. But unfortunately, as usually happens when you get a bit too complacent, we were soon caught out when we were walking through the caravans with our two new girlfriends. Who do you think just happened to be coming around the corner? You guessed it: Anne and Lynn. It didn't go down well as you can imagine, and we both got a well-deserved good roasting off the four girls as it dawned on them that they'd been taken for a ride, literally! I admit I felt bad about that incident as I'd really liked Anne and had let my raging hormones take over. They stormed off and left Ray-one and me standing like a pair of idiots next to someone's caravan, trying to look cool whilst feeling pretty rubbish for messing up what could have been a good thing. I missed Anne after that because I had hoped she might want to keep in touch with me and we could meet up again. You live and learn, I guess, and I certainly did that, many times over.

We spent the rest of that holiday swimming in the sea and avoiding the masses of jellyfish, not to mention the sharks that amazingly scour the North East coastline. We'd seen a few fins from afar but didn't think much of it at first until someone told us they were often seen. But that holiday was to be the first of many trips away for us as a group of lads and we'd often go off on camping trips to Weardale, carrying backpacks and several tents between us, lapping up the countryside with the sun on our backs as we walked for miles through fields and stunning scenery. On many of those trips I would encounter spirit activity and knew we were being looked after, especially when we got eaten alive by midges and then managed to pitch one of the tents on top of an ant hill. We even had to see the local doctor on that occasion as we'd been bitten so badly. But I just felt at ease knowing that we were being protected, perhaps by a spirit with a sense of humour, but all the same it was a good feeling knowing we were never alone.

Is There Anybody There?

One trip I will always remember vividly was when I was sat outside my tent one night and could have sworn I saw shapes moving about in the nearby trees. It could have been a trick of the moonlight, my mind playing tricks on me because I always had that feeling of being watched. But when I heard my name being called, I decided to investigate, part of me thinking one of the lads was having a good old laugh at my expense. In amongst the woodland was what seemed to be a discarded graveyard, most of the graves covered in foliage and so overgrown that it was almost impossible to make out any writing on the stones. The following day I told the others about what I'd discovered, and we all trampled into the woods and had a good look around, pulling back the overgrown roots and branches that had hidden the graves from view. Old and grey headstones appeared standing tall, guarding whoever had been buried beneath the earth. Worn inscriptions that we couldn't make out adorned each stone and on some, it was impossible for us to read names and dates. We felt like we were on the set of a horror movie as we all sheepishly stumbled around, uncovering moss and more foliage to see if we could decipher anything at all. As we stood there not really knowing of our next move, I heard what sounded like a growl coming from the trees and I turned to look at the others. Much to my relief, they'd heard it too, and we were now standing with eyes on stalks, mouths wide open, and frozen to the spot. When you get confronted with a situation like that, especially in the middle of an ancient burial site that's obviously been long forgotten over the years judging by the mess it was in, your mind tends to work overtime and after what felt like minutes of us eyeing the area up suspiciously, wondering if a zombie might jump out of one of the graves, we ran for dear life, back through the trees and to the safety of our tents. What a sight that must have been: A group of fitness fanatics with sixpacks and arrogance and an invincible attitude, bolting through the woods, resembling a group of screaming idiots running for cover from an old graveyard. Suffice to say, we moved our tents to a different pitch that afternoon, one where other campers had established themselves and looked quite at home sat around steel kettles on a gas stove. We got a few funny looks as we set up our own camp, still a bit shocked at the morning's antics, and I suppose we looked a bit pathetic as we got on with the job in mute silence, eager to hopefully enjoy the rest of our trip in peace. But we soon got settled and spent that night sat around the campfire trying not to think about the strange noise we'd heard earlier on in those woods.

Being young and reckless however, and dare I say it, glutton for punishment, we didn't stay down for too long and found ourselves having a walk the following day through the fields. The sun was shining as we were mooching through the tall grass, once more carefree and enjoying the freedom of youth, when we suddenly came across what appeared to be a derelict old house. It was your typical childhood drawing with a front door and a window either side, then two windows on the first floor. As we got nearer, we noticed the dilapidated state of it, paint peeling off the windowsills and the door looking like it was ready to fall off its hinges. But something we also noticed was an orchard at the side with apple and pear trees that seemed ripe for picking. Obviously tempted, we made our way closer to the garden area with every intention of filling our pockets with fresh fruit.

It was just as we got into the orchard that something caught my eye in one of the top floor windows of the house: The figure of what I thought was a man seemed to be watching us. It spooked me at first, especially after our experience the previous day, but I'd definitely seen someone. I turned to the others and mentioned that I thought we should knock on the door before we pick any fruit, the memory of my friends and I breaking into a private garden and stealing apples from the trees when I was five being at the forefront of my mind. Not too keen on my suggestion, they volunteered me to do the knocking and so off I went, feeling somewhat nervous underneath the boyish bravado front I had to put on for the others. Rayone came with me and together we knocked on the door. Unfortunately, we hadn't expected it to be quite so fragile and the bloody thing fell in, leaving us boys wondering if we'd knocked too hard whilst the others stood behind us doubled over with laughter.

"Is there anybody there?" I shouted, sticking my head inside and noticing how abandoned it looked. But when no one replied, we all decided to be brave and trudge on through, having a good nosey around, not that there was much to see apart from a few filthy sheets and some ancient tins in the kitchen area of which looked as though they could have contained food. The whole place was thick with dust and debris, rotten floorboards and spiders' webs, and it took some doing just to get to the bottom of the stairs. As we stood there looking up, wondering who would be first to venture, a movement in the corner of my eye caught my attention and I turned my head around quickly to see what I thought could have been the figure of a man. I have to admit that at this stage I wasn't sure whether to be spooked or excited about this house and made the decision to suggest to the lads that we do a séance. I wasn't scared of the spirit world, but I didn't want to encourage anything bad to happen, mainly for the fact I didn't want my friends to experience the less savoury aspects of the paranormal, but also because I had to stay calm and at least look like I was the brave one here. And so, after a few heads nodding and one or two answers of, "Yeah, why not?" we left the house to return to our campsite and then went back that night with a glass and a notepad that we'd written the twenty-six letters of the alphabet on, along with the words, '*Yes*' and '*No*'.

Haunted House

It felt like a bit of a trek going back to that house in the dark, retracing our steps and trying not to trip up as we all stalked through the fields with a couple of torches and the rucksack filled with our séance equipment. There was an excitement amongst us and even though an eerie atmosphere seemed to have descended over us all, we couldn't wait to get back to that derelict house and summon up the spirits. "I wonder if anyone will come through," Billy asked me, and I shrugged, not really wanting to enthuse his optimism too much just in case it was a waste of time. I still hadn't told them about the figure I'd seen at the upstairs window, or the figure of a man I caught standing at the doorway to the hall. If there *was* activity in that house, we would find it, I was quite sure of that. But I didn't want to put any thoughts in the lads' minds because I wanted them to experience it for themselves if someone were to try and make contact, without me pre-empting that it could happen. They'd have been too excited and would have taken every tiny sound to be something spiritual if they knew I was sure I'd seen something, and we all needed to concentrate rather than be sat there chattering about a creaky floorboard and a possible ghost in our midst.

We finally got to the house and climbed over the front door that Ray-one and I had knocked on earlier, that still lay looking pretty sorry for itself with some rather large splinters now protruding from it. "Shall we sit in the middle of the front room?" Ray-two asked, and I nodded. "Yeah, set the stuff down here," I said, shining my torch onto the floor that looked like someone had poured a bucket of dust over. I brushed some of it away to reveal what had probably been quite nice floorboards once upon a time but had definitely seen better days since whoever lived here had moved away.

Billy and John set the letters out in a circle whilst Ray-two took the glass out of the rucksack and placed it, upside down, in the middle. Me and Ray-one sat down and made ourselves comfortable, sitting cross-legged on the hard, filthy floor. We flinched a couple of times when an owl hooted outside and all looked around at each other, probably all wondering the same thing: What next?

As always, the others looked to me for guidance. "Everyone put your finger on the glass," I said, taking the lead as they followed. Five of us sat in a circle hunched over a makeshift Ouija board with our forefingers lightly touching a tumbler. "Does anyone want to communicate?" I asked out, looking around me at the shapes that danced on the walls as the tiniest speck of moonlight shone through to make a reflection. I was still hoping I hadn't been imagining the figure earlier on and that perhaps whoever it had been might visit us that night and make contact. We were a group of five eager young lads wanting a bit of excitement and something to happen and as we all looked at each other again, waiting for the adventure to begin, I felt the slightest movement of the glass beneath my fingertip. I didn't speak at first, knowing that if I'd felt it, then one of the others must have done, too. Then the glass started to move a bit more until Billy and Ray-two took their fingers away and just left me, John and Ray-one touching it. "Who's moving it?" they asked as we sat there trying not to look spooked and probably failing miserably. "It's not me," I said. "Is it you, John?" Ray-one asked, but John looked as shocked as we did and shook his head. "No, it isn't," he insisted. "Put your fingers back on it," I said to Billy and Ray-two, and they reluctantly did. "It's you," Ray-one said, directing his accusation at Billy as the glass started to move even more. But I knew it wasn't Billy, or any of them, because at that point I was starting to hear voices, and one in particular was the gruff sound of a man, perhaps, I thought to myself, the same one who I'd seen in the house earlier that day.

"Get out of the house!" he roared now, and the others looked around then started fidgeting. They'd heard it, too. We all sat there, desperate not to break the link, but also desperate to stand up and make a run for it, whilst none of us wanted to look like a sissy by going first.

"I've gone really hot," John said, lifting his shoulders and exhaling as though he was sat in a furnace. "Me, too," Billy said, as he, too, exhaled. The two Rays nodded and I agreed, feeling a burning sensation all over my back like there was a bonfire behind me. Unable to keep still, we all took our fingers off the glass which was now circling the Ouija board frantically. It took another few seconds for us to get back on our feet and charge for the front door, bolting through the apple and pear orchard and into the field again where we shone our torches to light the way back. The heat had dispersed and even though we were now a glass down and had left an empty rucksack in the house, we had no intention of going back to retrieve them. Making our way hastily back to the campsite, we came to the conclusion that the derelict house in the trees was haunted. And I knew for definite that I'd seen someone at that window, *and* at the doorway.

It turned out after speaking to the local shop owner the following day, that there had once been a fire inside the house and its occupants, a man and a woman, had died in that fire. The shop owner also told us that people had reported seeing faces at the windows and heard voices shouting out for help. We decided to stay around the campsite for the rest of that holiday and stay out of trouble for a change, hard as that was. But there was no way we were going anywhere near that house again!

The Camaraderie

As those teenage years melted away, I knew that before long I'd have to think about settling down, finding myself a proper job that might put me on the housing ladder one day. As a tear-away, I wasn't too keen on the inevitable responsibility I'd have to face, but my parents always encouraged me to get out into the big bad world and, in a nutshell, grow up. And so, my experience as a miner began a few years later when I was twenty-one. Three months training at Ashington Colliery and nine months provisional work in a coalmine that was just twenty-six inches high, led to ten years working as a miner, many of those years faced with claustrophobic and oppressive conditions carrying heavy equipment back and forth along a filthy, underground pit.

I made a lot of good friends in that job, some I'm still in touch with today. One in particular was a giant of a man at seven foot tall, totally out of place in such a confined working environment. But he was a good friend to me and on a few occasions helped me out when I'd get picked on. I could always stick up for myself, but my friendship with the gentle-giant, Frank, was cemented one time when he waded in and wrapped a strap around one guy's neck who was a complete bully, ordering him to leave me well alone. No one picked on me after that incident and Frank and I became good friends.

The working conditions in the mines were pretty dire in those days and it wasn't unusual for us to be expected to mine in three or four inches of filthy, stagnant water, and no doubt filled with all kinds of diseases. You took your life in your own hands just to walk away on a Friday afternoon with a little brown envelope filled with cash. Not enough cash in my opinion for what you were expected to do, but still, it was a job and in those days it was secure.

Unfortunately, my mouth got me into trouble eventually as I complained to the Union and management that there was a huge lack of equipment and the tools we were given weren't up to scratch. I got sacked for making the point, perhaps because they knew I was right and weren't prepared to do anything about it. They probably thought it was better to lose a miner than have one spouting about a lack of tools and raising awareness to the powers-that-be that the pit was unsafe and not fit for purpose. Their action to let me go resulted in the other miners being willing to go on strike, and that included miners from pits around the other Durham coalfields as well. As you can imagine it made me feel quite humble and proud that I'd had such an impact on so many people. I'm sure they were scared that if a miner had been sacked for making a valid point, then it would only happen again to someone else, and eventually I was offered my job back.

The camaraderie in that coal mine was second to none. Those days in the pit made me realise the value of true friends, not to mention colleagues who stick up for each other. And like many other people who have that kind of bond with their fellow men, I will always remember those days with fondness, albeit as we carried out painfully hard work.

The Perils Of Dutch Courage

One of the places I used to enjoy going to in my days down the pit was a nightclub called The Mitea. I'm sure you've all heard of Ant and Dec? Well, the club was situated in Benwell Village where they became famous as the kids of Byker Grove. Like most youngsters, I enjoyed a drink and a night out, some that often ended in a pub brawl or a scrap around the alleys after one too many. And this particular night was no exception. My nephew came to stay for a while and I took him to The Mitea, showing off my favourite club and hoping to introduce him to a few of the friends I used to hang out with. Unfortunately, we got separated in the club and there I was, propping up the bar, looking around for him when I suddenly noticed a group of lads giving a young girl what looked like a hard time. I've always considered myself a gentleman when it comes to the ladies, and I can't stand to see a woman being intimidated. So, I decided to approach them, maybe against my better judgement, but I knew I had to do it if I was to sleep easy that night.

As I got near, they turned around and looked me up and down, probably wondering why a guy on his own who looked like he couldn't fight his way out of a paper bag, would even think of taking them on. "Back off," I said, bravely, and their reply was to tell me to mind my own business before one of them pulled out a knife from inside his jacket. I have to say I was scared at this point, but I was also full of Dutch courage and my principles wouldn't allow me to just walk away without at least another few words slung in their direction. A couple of punches were exchanged, and fortunately the knife went back under the jacket before I eventually gave up and moved back to the bar.

Much to my irritation however, one of the gang members joined me at the bar and announced that he'd see me outside. I suppose the drink was talking as well as my confidence, but at two-fifteen in the morning I found myself standing outside, freezing to death, waiting for him to appear. Hopping from one foot to the other trying to keep warm and failing miserably, I huddled myself further inside my jacket before deciding to give up and begin my walk home, wondering where the hell my nephew had ended up. It was a quiet country road, no pavements and no streetlights, but I'd walked that road so often I could have got back home blindfolded.

It was when I saw the headlights coming towards me that my stomach turned, as I wondered who could be out at this unearthly hour in the morning, especially on such a deserted road. The car sped up as it got closer to me. With no pavement to walk on and nowhere to jump out of the way, the inevitable happened as it made contact with me, flinging me over the bonnet, and throwing me behind it in a crumpled heap. My first instinct was to get up and run away, but the fall had winded me and prevented me from getting up off the road for a few moments not knowing what had happened. It was just as I tried to move again when the driver's door and passenger door of the car opened and two guys jumped out, both of them brandishing a baseball bat, and approaching me before I had time to think of my next move.

Blow after blow hit me as they told me to stay down, their voices raised with venom as they beat me. I could feel the blood pouring down my face and seeping into my eyes and I tried to wipe it away only to be hit again. I can't remember seeing the knife, but they used it twice and even tried to gouge my eye out with it. The whole attack seemed to last forever, though was probably only a few minutes of them raining down their worst blows to try and keep me incapacitated. I couldn't have got up even if they'd let me. I was completely exhausted, bleeding from just about everywhere with excruciating pain flooding through my body. And then, to my horror, they got back into the car, put it in reverse and backed into me, leaving my jacket hooked to something underneath as they changed gear and began to drive forward. It wasn't long before the car stopped again, giving me time to unhook the jacket and have a look around. They'd driven back the nightclub - about 300 yards up the road I'd just walked down - and left me there. I was relieved to see the car drive away, but I knew I was in pretty bad shape and needed help as quickly as possible.

Fortunately for me, someone had seen me lying on the floor outside the club and managed to flag down a police car. I can't say why, at half-two in the morning, a police car and a witness just happened to be in that particular area the same time that I was being attacked, but I can only assume my Guides were with me once again. An ambulance was called and I was rushed to the nearest hospital where I was very close to being pronounced dead. My pulse was extremely faint, but a duty doctor managed to pick it up and subsequently had me charged down to ICU on a trolley. They were very dark times for me, and it took a further two years of intensive treatment to get me back to some kind of normality.

It wasn't all bad however, as I met my first wife during that time of having treatment and so it did give me some hope. The guys who had attacked me were found and charged and sentenced to twenty years between them. That was a result in itself. At least they'd be off the streets, I thought. I'll never forget, whilst watching them being taken down, how their families shouted insults at me, saying, "You're dead," when my wife's Uncle David shouted back at them, "If anything happens to that lad, you'll be the dead ones."

You see, my wife came from one of Newcastle's most notorious families, a family that people simply didn't mess with. My attackers didn't know I'd married into that family at the time and when Uncle David made them aware at the sentencing, they realised it wouldn't do them any good to come after me. I wished I could have filmed the surprised looks on their faces that day; it would have kept me entertained for a long time!

My injuries sustained from that night at the club, unfortunately, prevented me from going back to work in the pit. I'd spent ten years working there, and made some good friends throughout that time, but I had to leave and start looking for a new job that would be less labour-intensive and a little kinder to my body. Still in my twenties, it felt quite tough to know I'd have to start again because of a violent attack where I'd had no chance of defending myself against baseball bats and a knife. But such was my life back then and my wife and I made a temporary move to Jersey, before returning to Tyne and Wear a few months later. I was lucky enough to land a job on the Metro for two years, whilst having a second job to top up my income working in Uncle David's nightclub collecting glasses. I sometimes worked behind the bar too, and on occasion I had a go at DJ'ing. But eventually, the club was raided by the police and things went downhill from then.

Sadly, my marriage to Dawn ended in 1984. We did have a son together: Leighton, who was born in 1981, and I often feel proud when people say he looks like me and has my mannerisms. A couple of years after my divorce was really the time when my spiritual work began, after an experience that changed things irrevocably...

Hot Stuff

It was the latter part of 1986 when I called at my mother's house one day and found her sat at the kitchen table chatting to her good friend, Molly. As a practicing medium, I'd always admired Molly and been intrigued by her in equal measure. Something I always remember her for was the scented oil that used to invisibly emit from her hands as though she'd smothered it over them time and again. I sat in the lounge that day whilst Mum and Molly made tea in the kitchen, enjoying the sunny climate and blue sky from my chair at the window.

Sitting there peacefully for five or ten minutes, suddenly, to my shock, Molly barged into the lounge seeming to have been possessed. She looked spooked, afraid, and as though someone was pushing her towards me, even though there was only the two of us in the room. As she stood within inches from my face, she lifted her hand and placed it on my forehead. I then heard a hissing sound before a strange energy sensation travelled through my entire body, reaching my head where Molly's hand was resting. It all happened so quickly and was over just as fast, leaving me questioning what on earth had just happened and leaving Molly stood back in surprise.

The following day at home, I started to hear voices and see outlines of people in the room, and a weird, hazy light penetrated through the air. Naturally, I thought I was going crazy and wondered if I'd drunk too much the night before, but then I got really hot and the sensation of being burnt suddenly overwhelmed me. My hands felt like they were on fire, and I remember picking up my nana's Bible only to see the pages become scorched by the heat on my fingers. It was the middle of winter, snow lay on the ground as huge flakes continued to fall, and there was I, walking around outside bare chested as though I was on holiday abroad in 40-degree heat! Something strange was happening to me, that was for sure, as my head seemed to illuminate the way. It was like I was wearing a miner's lamp, only the light emanating from it was ten-times stronger.

Knowing I needed answers as to what the hell was happening to me, I made my way to the local Catholic church where I sat with Father O'Connell for a while. I wasn't a Catholic and had to come clean, but he took sympathy on me and led me into the vestry where he said a few prayers and drew the symbol of the cross on my forehead with his finger. He explained to me that I'd been given the 'Kundalini Awakening', which is a practice that enlightens your spiritual being. He gave me some information about the process, of which he swore me to secrecy, and then advised me to get myself a large steak and a pint of beer and then think about grounding myself. I have to admit that at the time I didn't have a clue what he was talking about and right then I didn't really care. I just wanted to feel normal again.

I hadn't slept properly for more than three months, and I was exhausted. But I managed to find my way to the nearest pub where I took Father O'Connell's advice and ordered myself a steak meal and a welcome pint of beer. The landlord apologised to the few punters that hovered around the bar explaining that the boiler had broken that day, which was especially annoying in the middle of winter. But a friend of mine, Lester, who was stood propping up the bar next to me, was clearly perspiring like he was unable to stand the heat. "It's red hot in 'ere," he commented, "have you fixed the boiler, then?" The landlord shook his head. "No, mate," he confirmed. It was obvious I was still radiating heat so much so that Lester looked like he was ready to pass out!

I drank my pint and ordered another and am very pleased to say I slowly started to cool down, probably much to Lester's relief. I could feel the heat leaving my body as each pint was consumed, suffice to say I had a fair few that afternoon!

A Satisfied Audience

*F*ollowing that strange event, I continued to experience more phenomena over the next few months as I managed to control my Kundalini Awakening and began to practice spiritual healing. My work had started, and I found myself on a mission to help people. Perhaps it was my 'calling'; I'd like to believe it was.

My first healing work was at a cancer support group who had asked on a local radio station for anyone in the healing business to come forward and offer their services. I wanted to do this; I felt I *needed* to do this. And so, I took myself to a place called Riding Mill where I met Joan Ridley, who ran a group for cancer patients wanting and needing to feel they could recover from the nightmare they were currently living through. Joan herself, was in remission. Even though I enjoyed going along to the group meetings, I never practiced my healing on anyone there, but I did make some good friends, two of them being Vera and Dougie Bateman who ran a spiritualist church nearby. The couple were both mediums and invited me along to their church where they helped me train as a spiritual healer. These lovely people encouraged me completely to learn and succeed in my work and I can honestly say I owe them so much.

One day, Vera asked if I'd like to take part in their 'Development' classes with the potential of becoming a practicing medium in the same context as themselves. Of course, I did, it was my life now and I was delighted to start those classes and be a part of their fascinating world. We had such a lot of fun, albeit learning and developing a gift that I knew had been bestowed upon me in my childhood days. The classes took place in a pitch-dark room where we couldn't even see our hands in front of our faces. There was usually about twelve of us in the class, all sat in seats positioned around a circular table. One evening, I was feeling mischievous and the child in me took over when I started to tap the person to me on their shoulder.

She swung around, not knowing what or who had touched her, and screamed, "Oh my god!" to the room of shocked people. Then I put my knees underneath the table and started to lift it slowly. I know I shouldn't have done it, but the laugh we had as everyone shot off their seats and ran like the clappers for the door was priceless. They really were such fun times.

After a few sessions, Dougie told me he'd like me to take a service one night: "Get up on the rostrum," he said, "and show 'em what you're made of." I wasn't sure I was ready, I'll be honest, but I agreed to do it anyway and spent the next few days in a panic hoping Sunday evening would never come round.

It did, of course, and I found myself shaking like a leaf, dressed up to the nines, and scouring a congregation of around seventy people all there to see a newcomer hopefully impress them by doing his stuff on the stage in front of them. It was nerve-racking. All those faces looking in my direction as Dougie introduced me before he sat down. I thought my legs might give way as I stood up and cleared my throat, thinking about what I'd rehearsed the past few days. But, as always, I should have known better than to waste time rehearsing when my job now was to pass on messages from the spirit world to this mesmerised audience who sat before me, all hoping one of the messages I received would be for them.

I managed it, I'm pleased to say, however much I stumbled and shook and prayed the messages I conveyed would all make sense. As I got a bit more into it, I could feel the nervousness abating, and it actually became fun. It had turned out to be an uplifting experience doing my first stage reading that was, fortunately for me, well-received. I knew that speaking in front of people was something I became good at, and as time went on, I found myself excited at the prospect of relaying information to those seeking clarification from the other side that their loved ones really did still exist somewhere else.

Visit From An Angel

When I was about thirty, I remember visiting my mother quite late one night. We sat in her lounge together watching the television. Back in those days, the TV would go off in the early hours, and it must have been around two-am, when Mum had gone to bed, that I recall what I can only describe as a haze descending over my eyes. Assuming I must have been over-tired, I lay down on the sofa hoping I might drift off.

Lying there, wondering if sleep would indeed come, my eyes averted to my left where my mum had positioned a vase of flowers. As if invisible hands were touching the flowers, two white roses were lifted from the vase and placed on the sofa at the side of me. It would have been enough to scare any living being to death, but for some reason I felt absolutely no fear whatsoever, just a calmness and a warm feeling that seemed to envelop me all of a sudden.

Relaxed, I closed my eyes, expecting to see just darkness as I would no doubt fall asleep. But what I did see will stay with me for the rest of my life:

I could still see the light of the room, the two armchairs and the coffee table, my mum's sideboard and the electric fire. The vase of flowers was still sat on the table and the white roses still rested at my side. When I heard a voice calling out my name, my heart began to race, but my eyes stayed closed. I struggled to breathe, a sudden overwhelming feeling of no longer being alone having taken over. And then I heard the voice again. It was a man's voice that I'd never heard before: "Relax," it said, "nothing is going to hurt you."

My heart might have been going like the clappers, but I felt a strange sense of calm wash over me and I began to relax again. I opened my eyes a little and strained to look at the clock on the mantel piece: two-thirty-am. When I closed my eyes once more, I saw him; a man dressed like a Zulu Warrior holding a huge spear in his right hand and dressed in a skirt that looked to be made of grasses. He was standing to attention in the doorway of my mum's front room as though guarding it. "Who are you?" I asked, noticing the headdress he wore was now glowing a bright light in my direction.

As I sat up on the sofa, I continued glaring at this man that had invited himself into my mum's house, standing tall before me, and without further ado, the room suddenly started to change its appearance. No longer could I see the armchairs and the sideboard, but instead I was looking at other people dressed in Arabian attire with headbands and prominent costumes as though they'd travelled far and wide to see me. One person wore a long red cassock, golden hair falling loosely down his back and a pair of sandals on his feet.

"Brother," he said to me, in a voice which I thought I recognised. It was as though we knew each other well and him being in this room with me was all perfectly normal.

Just as I got my head around that scene, I was faced with another as I turned to see a porthole appear in the wall and the planet Earth on the other side of it. It was all so bizarre, yet it felt natural at the same time. I looked through the porthole at our blue and white planet and remember asking, "What about all the people on Earth?" The man in the red cassock told me, "They will destroy themselves as they have done before." I had no idea what he meant, and asked, "Can we not help to change their direction?" and was met with the response: "You can bring home as many as you can."

I never really understood that at the time, and not for a good while afterwards, but I think perhaps I do now. It was after this communication that I saw what seemed to be a doorway radiating a bright, white light. I started to feel like I was a young boy again, mischievous and invincible, and I manoeuvred myself and stuck my feet through the doorway. But at that point a sudden fear washed over me, one I hadn't experienced before. To my left I saw a figure standing looking at me. He was tall, dressed in a white robe and had two mysterious-looking bumps on each of his shoulders. As I continued to watch him, one of the bumps suddenly began to grow until a wing materialised and covered me, its golden light glowing against me as it wrapped itself around my body. I felt comforted and safe, secured in the knowledge that somehow, I was being protected. Any fear I might have had earlier on dissipated and left me languished in this incredibly fantastical encounter.

I had experienced the feeling of being reborn.

Within moments of that happening to me, I seemed to open my eyes again and revisit the familiarity of my mum's lounge; the coffee table and the armchairs and the sideboard all back to where they had been originally positioned. The man in the red cassock and the Zulu Warrior had vanished, and the vase of flowers once more graced the table with my mum's favourite roses all perfectly arranged. I glanced at the clock again and noticed it was now four-thirty-am. Two and a half hours of my life had been taken and even though people will assume I'd fallen asleep and been dreaming of a land far away, I know that experience was very real.

Believe me, I used to be incredibly sceptical and would question anything out of the ordinary, but when my mum came into the lounge four hours later and exclaimed, "Oh my god, have you seen your face?" I looked in the mirror and noticed the burn down my left cheek. Not wanting to worry my worried-looking mum, I took her advice and went to see my doctor who told me that kind of mark was like sunburn. "Radiation burns," he said, "something we tend to get after sitting in the sun for prolonged periods of time."

It was the middle of winter, and it was freezing outside. And even Doctor Drinkwater didn't have an explanation for *that* diagnosis.

Spiritual Healing

I went on to further my spiritual healing career soon after. My work took me to many different places where I would talk to people about the importance of healing the soul and how once that had happened, the body would heal itself. I came across many healers throughout my life, from several different backgrounds and with various methods on how to conduct their own healing. One person, amongst many that I admired, was a boxer and a fireman called George Chapman, who became a psychic surgeon. He would work on people's eyes and delve into other illnesses they had, working alongside medical professional, Doctor Lang. I became good friends with George's son, Michael, who was a full-time healer and owned clinics all around the world.

I have had the pleasure to know some very well-known healers in my time, as well as Michael: John Cain, Harry Edwards and Stephen Turoff were all successful in their field and it's been a great honour to be able to call these people my friends. Their influence was hugely encouraging for me as I took myself to many different towns all over the UK and helped people through my work. I ran workshops and gave lectures about the secrets of healing and how it became so important to me. I'd answer a wealth of questions as people wanted to know more, their interest being spiked as they'd get to know me as a genuine healer. I guess my reputation was building back then and I met more and more people who not only needed my spiritual healing, but wanted to know more about it, too.

One lady brought her husband to see me. He had walking problems, though I can't recall exactly what they were. But when I saw him, I told him to close his eyes and just relax. "You aren't getting your teeth out today," I joked, hoping it might break the ice and make him feel less nervous. Then, all of a sudden, a bolt of light materialised out of nowhere seeming to penetrate all through the man's body. His lips turned blue, and it honestly looked like he'd passed over. His wife, a retired nurse, was naturally mortified and flapped her arms, screaming that he'd stopped breathing and someone must do something. "He'll be fine," I assured her, knowing that before long he would be back with us in the land of the living, most probably wanting to recall his experience.

When he came round and his wife finally got over the shock, the man began to tell us that he'd seen a blinding light and had been transported to another place where he felt comforted. He went on to say he felt no pain and that there was a figure standing in front of him calming him down. What he'd experienced was spiritual healing; his soul having been healed. Once he realised this, he no longer felt the pain in his legs and was able to walk without aids. I never saw him or his wife again after that night.

~ ❖ ~

Those early years of spiritual healing in my thirties were very inspiring for me. I really enjoyed my work and looked forward to meeting new people as I continued to travel around the country. I was making quite a name for myself too, and so decided to embark on a business course in the hope of becoming more familiar with computers, which were starting to take over and become the new age of technology. I enrolled myself onto a government-based course for a year whilst also working part-time at a health centre is Jesmond as a healer. This all came about after doing some work at a doctor's surgery and then being invited to give a talk at Newcastle University.

Some patients were beyond physical help, having been diagnosed with terminal illnesses or conditions that simply had no cure. I was approached by GPs who would refer these patients to me, perhaps as some kind of experiment, and I would set about trying to help them as much as was possible. Whilst doing this work, I was fortunate enough to meet a wonderful lady called Trisha and as time went on, we realised our paths had meant to cross. I fell in love with Trisha and eventually we moved in together. She was everything to me back then. We laughed and talked to each other and hardly had a cross word. Life was content and full of joy, and I became a very happy man.

I remember one funny memory involving Trisha when I went on a night out with my good friend, Dave. We paraded around Newcastle City Centre, in and out of the pubs until it was closing time and I had to get the last bus back before I'd end up passed out drunk in an alleyway in Haymarket. There I was, sat on the top deck, fast asleep. Predictably, I missed my stop and ended up at Blyth Bus Station, miles away from home in Seaton Burn. It would be hours before I got home now as I'd have no choice but to walk all the way back.

That walk home took me past some roadworks and being as drunk as I was, I lost my footing and went headfirst into a deep pothole. I was absolutely covered in mud and was freezing cold. When I managed to clamber out, completely caked, I must have looked like a madman on a mission, and it's just lucky I didn't come across anyone on the rest of my walk, especially a policeman!

It was five that morning when I finally landed at our house and as you can imagine, Trisha wasn't best pleased. I copped a few lectures for that, not to mention being covered in mud and bringing dirty shoes inside. But we laughed about it afterwards, as we often laughed about most things that weren't worth getting upset over.

The only drawback to my work in those days was that it took me away from Trisha for nights on end. My healing support often took me to London and its surrounding areas. I enjoyed it, as I always did, but I didn't enjoy being away from my girl. She was so patient with me and respected that my work would always take me away from time to time, and for that I loved her even more.

It was one day when I was at home helping with the housework that Trisha fell over a chair and lay on the floor clutching her right side. She complained that her rib cage was in pain and said she was breathless, so without hesitation I took her to the doctor's surgery. He wasn't happy to just give her an explanation or make a diagnosis there and then, and instead sent her for a scan to the local hospital. That was to be the start of a very difficult time in my life, for soon after that scan took place, Trisha was diagnosed with cancer.

Understandably, our world fell apart. Her prognosis wasn't good, and she was told the cancer was in its advanced stages. She'd been fine until falling over that damned chair and then our lives crumpled around us. It was devastating. The doctors said there was nothing they could do and would only offer her chemotherapy, which, they pointed out, would only prolong her life, not cure the cancer. I was utterly bereft. Here I was, a healer and unable to do nothing to heal the love of my life. I put all my strength into nursing her over the next few months, watching as she deteriorated before my eyes. Seeing how weak she was becoming during that time ripped my heart out and I'd never felt so helpless in all my entire life.

We had good days, of course, and there were times that she'd feel stronger than she did on other days, wanting to carry on as normal as was possible. And on those stronger days, she insisted I carried on with my work whilst she always gave me her support. I'd take her back and forth to the hospital for treatment and I'd work in between, but eventually she was admitted to St Oswald's Hospice in Gosforth where she would stay and receive palliative care. I visited her every day, getting to know the staff and other patients that were interested in my healing abilities, and I was always happy to offer them some spiritual healing if they wanted it. Some of them said they felt better afterwards and even though that gave me a great deal of satisfaction, I couldn't ever feel good about my work whilst Trisha was in that hospice knowing there was no hope for her. I couldn't help her. And that pain ripped through me twenty-four hours a day.

During a fairly good spell in the hospice when I felt confident about leaving Trisha in the capable hands of the staff, I took a plane to London having had quite a few bookings at the clinic where I practiced there. It was a weekend, so a little quieter to commute. But when I got to the clinic that afternoon, I suddenly felt a wave of anxiety wash over me and I knew I had to get back to Newcastle and back to Trisha. I got a taxi to the hospice straight from the airport and was told upon walking through the door that Trisha was unresponsive and had fallen into a coma.

The nurse took me to her room where I sat myself down in a highbacked armchair next to the bed, holding her hand and stroking her face softly, telling her how much I loved her. She looked peaceful as she lay there, as though she was listening to me and taking it all in. The kind nurses put another bed in the room and positioned it next to Trisha's so that I could lie next to her. I knew there would be no coming back from this, but just to be lying alongside my beautiful girl and the best friend I'd ever had meant everything to me as I reminisced about the fun we'd had together and the connection we'd shared, that we would no doubt continue to share in the next life.

I would have given my life for hers. It was that simple. The pain that coursed through me whilst having to sit and watch her deteriorate was excruciating, and at five-am the next morning, my beautiful Trisha passed away. I honestly think that was the hardest experience of my life, but I knew I had to go on living and she wouldn't have wanted me to wallow in self-pity. Trisha's daughter was fourteen at the time of her mum's passing and we helped each other through many dark days. Trisha was only forty-six years old; far too young to join the world of spirit. I still miss her and think about her often, and I know she's watching over me and will continue to do so. We must always accept that life goes on, but we should never forget the events of our past that mould us into the person we are today.

Mixing With The Stars

By the time I reached the age of forty, I worked in Watford as a spiritual healer and had made many friends through the work I carried out. I'd attend regular conferences and courses, and on one occasion I attended a seminar that some of my healer friends were hosting at the Sherlock Hotel on Baker Street in London. It was being run in order to find new recruits for their business, NSA Water Filters, and I was pleasantly surprised to see a relatively large amount of people interested enough to attend.

My eyes strayed to the back of the room at one point, to a lady who looked extremely familiar, and whom I couldn't help but think I'd seen on TV. I shook myself off, continuing to glance over occasionally, trying to put a name to her face, but gave up after a while in favour of supporting my friends and their seminar.

Later that day, we all went to a nearby tea rooms to enjoy a welcome break in the proceedings that we felt we deserved. As we walked through the door, the staff suddenly started to fuss around us, making me assume they were excited at seeing a large group of people grace their shop, and I even wondered if it was me that they were excited to see! My ego must have been pretty big back then and I watched as they hurried around, moving tables and chairs to accommodate us. We sat down and I noticed how the staff couldn't take their eyes away from the mysterious woman who'd been sat at the back of the room earlier, the same one I'd tried in vain to put a name to after being convinced I'd seen her before.

I couldn't resist it; my curiosity got the better of me and I eventually plucked up the courage to talk to her. "I've seen you somewhere before," I said, and she simply replied by telling me she didn't know me and that she never forgets a face. That was the end of the conversation and I smiled and went back to my seat, even more puzzled than I was before!

As we finished afternoon tea and filtered out of the café, I noticed, once again, everyone watching her as though amazed at her being amongst our group. We walked towards our waiting cars and she began to rub her neck as though she was in some discomfort, to which I asked, "Are you okay?" She shook her head and carried on massaging the area I assumed was troubling her, and replied, "I fell off a horse and got whiplash."

As a healer, I've always found it hard to see someone suffering if I think I can help them, which is why it was so very hard to watch Trisha go through what she did, because I knew there was nothing I could do to help her. But my natural instinct was always to help that person and before I knew it, I'd offered to help this lady by inviting her to my friend's house in London where I would try and heal her neck.

"Are you a therapist?" she asked. I shook my head in reply and explained that I'm a spiritual healer. I was thrilled when she agreed to come over that following Sunday morning to see what I could do.

She turned up in an extremely nice car. It was expensive and not one that was seen often back in those days. She looked particularly elegant wearing what I could only describe as more upmarket attire that hugged her slim figure, and she seemed to light up the hallway as she entered the house, allowing me to lead her into my therapy room. It was then when she introduced herself properly to me: Hayley Mills.

Wow, I thought, *Hayley Mills is standing in front of me*. I was in awe at this incredibly iconic actress who's so famous and beautiful and who'd even won a Golden Globe award for New Star of the Year Actress. I guess you could say I was star-struck for a moment, and I had to compose myself to return back to the here and now. It didn't enter my thoughts that her father was Sir John Mills and most of her family were in the film industry, too. Some of the films she has starred in over the years have included *Whistle Down the Wind*, *Tiger Bay*, and Disney's *Pollyanna*. I couldn't believe I hadn't put a name to her face before now. Although, without the film makeup and the big screen flare, she had still appeared as a stunning and sophisticated lady who was trying to mingle into the background. *Too famous for that*, I thought, *this lady is a true legend*.

She made herself comfortable on the chair and I slowly began to work my magic on her neck. To say I was nervous was an understatement! Unfortunately, she noticed my hands were shaking and pointed it out. "Is that the energy going through your hands?" she asked. "No," I replied, "I'm nervous!"

After asking me why, I told her that I hadn't expected to be giving healing to an iconic actress whilst in London this weekend, and she smiled and replied very graciously,

"Don't be silly. We are all the same only we have different roles to play in life. We are all on a different path." It broke the ice, much to my relief, and our conversation began to flow as my hands eventually stopped shaking. I even asked her, "When do you get paid?" and she replied, "On a Friday, just like you." She was a truly lovely lady, and really, quite down to earth for someone who was idolised by many throughout the world.

That first encounter with Hayley Mills led to many more and she kindly invited me to her home in Middlesex, an old coaching house in its own grounds with a wonderful expanse of perfectly manicured lawns and areas of natural beauty. I was once again in awe as I drove up to it and she greeted me as I got out of my car then took me to a seating area in the garden where she introduced me to her son, Crispian Mills - he used to be the lead singer in a popular psychedelic rock band called *Kula Shaker*, during the 1990s.

Hayley even invited me to stay overnight one time, of which I did, feeling particularly honoured at being in her beautiful home. I remember coming down the stairs during that stay and walking into the lounge to a sight that took my breath away. Sir John Mills was standing in front of the TV, and I just about managed to stutter the words, "Good morning, Sir John," before he smiled and said, "My friends call me Johnny." It was like being in a very ordinary house with an ordinary family, and even though I spent the duration of my time there feeling completely star-struck and somewhat lost for words, it was a wonderful experience to meet such incredible people and be able to call them my friends.

Sir John had one of the early mobile phones back then and later that day, as we were having lunch on the lawn whilst discussing all sorts of topics from healing to films, and spirit guides to BAFTA awards, he took a phone call from the one and only, Burt Lancaster, almost sending me into a frenzy of surreality. When he then went on to say, "I'm sitting in my daughter's garden having a spot of lunch with Noel," I'm surprised I didn't choke on my cucumber sandwiches! I wasn't that well known back then, and certainly not famous, so I imagine Mr Lancaster was quite puzzled on the other end of the phone wondering who on early 'Noel' was.

To add the icing on the cake, Sir John invited me to his home in Denham Village, a charming Tudor mansion that I couldn't wait to visit. My connections to the rich and famous were only just beginning...

Never Refuse A Pint

I guess I was now mixing with some extremely influential people and my life sometimes felt a little surreal, but in a good way. The honour of meeting and being associated with such famous people, as the ones I'd already encountered, was started to dawn on me and I loved the fact they wanted to get to know me as much as I them.

One of the best friends I have made over the years is the English Champion Badminton player, Derek Talbot MBE, whom I got to know through my work, and then by pure coincidence, over thirty-four years ago. Derek's mother, Gwen, came across an article about my spiritual healing in the local newspaper and decided to contact me to make an appointment to see her son. I didn't know who he was back then, and I went to visit their house, taking my friend, David, with me. When we arrived, we saw this chap jogging along the path leading up to the house in Kirkwhelpington, a picturesque village near Hexham in the North East, and David stopped in his tracks as we approached.

"That's the sport's guy, Derek Talbot," he pointed out, "he's a famous badminton player." I shrugged and carried on walking towards the house. "Never heard of him," I replied. We continued to the front door and Derek followed us in, then led us to a room where I began my work. He seemed like a really nice guy, down to earth and friendly, and I felt I'd done a good job in helping him.

Not long after that initial appointment, I decided to try and find some suitable premises to work from on a more permanent basis, and I started to look around the Newcastle area for something I could easily afford. I scoured the local papers, drawing rings around different places that looked affordable and would offer enough space, and then came across an advert for a manager at a new health centre in the exact area I wanted. The centre was due to be opened soon. It was a job I fancied at the time as I was also searching for some part-time work to tide me over financially, to top up the money I earned from healing. Plus, I thought it might lead me to being able to use a room there for my healing practices. So, I set about writing the letter, totally bigging myself up and making me sound like I was massively over-qualified for the job; in other words, I fudged quite a lot of it because I really did think it could be ideal for me. I wrote the address on the envelope, noting it was a P.O. Box, put a first-class stamp on it and then popped it in the post.

A few days later, whilst having a walk through the town, I just happened to bump into Derek and we stood on the pavement for a while, chatting. "Fancy going for a pint, Noel?" he asked. I nodded, never one to turn down a pint. "I need to stop off at my office first and pick up the mail," he added, and off we went, heading towards the building where his office was. I followed him inside where he collected his mail from a pigeon-hole, and then he led me into his office where I watched him rummage through it all, discarding the junk mail and putting the letters in a pile. I imagined he'd get fan mail every day, being as well-known as he was, and it crossed my mind that some of those handwritten letters were probably from adoring fans who admired watching him play badminton. And then, much to my surprise, he picked up an envelope with familiar writing on the front that I recognised as my own!

I stood there, my heart in my mouth, wondering why he'd have my letter, addressed to a P.O. Box, in his possession, and then he started opening it. I'm sure he didn't see the expression on my face, because if he had, he would have said something like, *"You okay?"* He pulled my letter out of the envelope and started reading it, nodding and making a few '*Hmm*' sounds as I continued watching. "This chap has a lot of qualifications," he said, "he looks interesting." Then he noticed the name on the letter and added, "I know that name." He hadn't registered it was me and put the letter down on the desk then picked out a few more and opened those, too. "I'll contact this one," he said, reaching for my letter again, and then he looked at me, his eyes wide as it suddenly dawned on him who the letter was from. He smiled and I smiled and all I could think was, *Thank God he's seen the funny side of it!*

"I had no idea I was writing to you," I said, probably looking a bit embarrassed by now. "I was looking for premises to work from and came across the job advert, and because I need to increase my income right now, I thought I'd apply." He laughed and nodded and said, "You can work from here." I was thrilled and we sorted the rent out there and then. And fortunately, we did manage to go for that pint!

Journey To Ibiza

My new friendship with Derek Talbot blossomed. A truly great guy, I felt privileged to know him personally and took an interest in his work as a Vibrational Practitioner. He was also a coach and a television presenter and worked with a man called Jack Temple, a well-known healer who carried out his own practices using herbs. Jack's reputation preceded him, showing incredible results on people from all walks of life from Royalty to movie stars and sport's personalities. Derek was hugely interested in the work Jack offered and became a student to these practices, trained by Jack himself. Jack's work often took him to different parts of the world where he'd discover cures for various ailments and eventually Derek qualified as a practitioner under Jack's tutorage. I had great respect for them both and for all that they achieved.

When Derek invited me to Ibiza with him in 1993, in order to promote a health centre he'd bought, I jumped at the chance. The centre was called 'Amara' and I couldn't wait to get there. When we arrived, I was whisked away to a radio station and interviewed on air, as well as being featured in magazines and newspapers, promoting my spiritual healing. It was a week-long fest of healing demonstrations and talking to various journalists and radio presenters about my work, and as it quickly took off, my live audience increased to between 100 and 200 people. Some that came to me were healed straight away, whilst others took a bit longer. But it was all an incredible experience for me, and the week went much too quickly. Before I knew it, the time came when I had to board a plane home, where I spent all the journey back planning my next visit.

Suffice to say, the success of that week prompted me to book a couple of weeks there again in November of that same year. We had a busy schedule booked consisting of workshops and talks, demonstrations and interviews, and I was delighted to arrive back in Ibiza with two weeks to look forward to, doing exactly what I loved so much. Derek had rented a villa in the hills with incredible panoramic views; mountains and little white fincas dotted about the countryside for as far as the eye could see. Word had got round, and we became inundated with enquiries, creating a buzz of excitement at the prospect of so many people turning up just for us – crowds in their hundreds on some occasions.

Our love for a pint and a night out took us to the famously known, '*Pacha's Nightclub*' in Ibiza Town one night. You can imagine the level of alcohol we consumed; we weren't lightweights! On the way back, walking up the hill towards the rented villa, stars lit up the inky-blue sky and the beautiful scenery around us. It was a breath-taking sight and I pointed upwards, slurring my words and swaying unsteadily on my feet as I said to Derek: "Look at those stars." He looked up to where I was pointing and unfortunately lost his balance, toppling over into a hole that just happened to be in our path. I looked down at my feet, searching around me, wondering if that last pint had been one too many, before asking, "Derek, where've you gone?"

I heard a few moans coming from nearby and started to drunkenly move my legs about, trying to steady myself whilst still working out why I was now swaying on a hillside by myself when only seconds earlier I'd been looking up at the stars with my buddy. And then the evitable happened. My twenty-four-stone bulk lost its footing and fell into the same bloody hole that Derek was trying to scramble out of, only he broke my fall and I landed smack-bang on top of him. If anyone had been around to see it, I reckon it could have won us an Oscar for Best Comedy Performance!

Derek, being quite a trendy guy, seemed more bothered about the designer gear he was wearing and the fact he'd landed on a cactus plant, probably ripping his shirt and trousers to shreds. We lay there for a while, getting our breaths back and wondering how the hell we were supposed to get out and continue our journey up the hill towards the villa. I can't say it was unpleasant lying in that hole with Derek and looking up at the starlit sky, the night enclosed around us as we shuffled about trying to avoid being pricked to death by a cactus plant, but we knew we needed to get out somehow and sober up!

You'd think I'd have had my fill of climbing hills after all the walking up and down we did from that villa to the town, but for my sins, a day or two later, I accepted an invitation to climb a mountain on the small island of 'Es Vedra', just off the coast of Ibiza. The mountain on the island is like a giant crystal reaching out of the sea and consists of a top layer of dirt that collected sixty-five million years ago. It's an actual formation of a geological tumble that happened one hundred and fifty-five million years ago, and the humming sound you can hear as you're standing on it gives off an eerie atmosphere as you look around and see just the deep blue ocean below. There's no beach or landing points and the only way we could get onto the island was by waiting for the boat to be carried along on a sudden wave towards the edge where we had to grab the rock and pull ourselves up onto a ledge. It was quite a challenge, but an adventure not to missed, nonetheless.

Uninhabited by human life, back then it was home to a herd of wild goats and the Ibizan black lizard. (The goats were unfortunately slaughtered by the government in 2016 to protect the island's fauna.) However, there are legends about the island that suggest it was used as a sacrificial base and another legend that tells us an old monk lived there known as The Carmelite Friar Francis Palau y Quer. He supposedly arrived on the island in 1855, having sailed from Barcelona, and spent a full week meditating and surviving on only rainwater, so the legend says. The rainwater, according to the story, came from drips in a cave formed three-hundred years ago. The island does have its own climate and whilst it might be raining and cloudy on Ibiza, it could be sunny and warm on Es Vedra.

We finally reached the summit where the cave had formed and had a look around it. It was damp and perhaps somewhat oppressive to anyone who didn't appreciate the calmness of forgotten times. We noticed how the pots that had caught the rainwater over the years, were still in place having been preserved, probably for mad mountain climbers like me and Derek to find. It really was a sight for sore eyes and not surprising that the monk had wanted to spend a week here meditating and hoping he could survive on rainwater and prayers. The atmosphere was so tranquil. We could hear the waves lapping against the rocks and the humming that seemed so mesmerising, and we could easily have stayed there for hours.

The other climbers - there were five of us altogether - had brought rucksacks containing a total of eleven bottles of wine. That was quite a lot between five, but as we didn't like wastage, we managed to get through them all whilst sat in that cave. Of course, we were all pretty tipsy by the time the last bottle had been consumed and it was now a case of having to climb back down to meet the fishing boat that was collecting us at the bottom.

We swayed and stumbled a few times, and one or two lost their balance, but we made it eventually and clambered into the boat to begin our ride back to the main island of Ibiza. "It's a good job you came back down that side of the mountain," one of the fishermen said to us on our journey back, "there's a storm raging on the other side." It was strange to think that different weather could form from one side of Es Vedra to the other, but it did. The whole experience had been phenomenal and one I'll never forget for the rest of my life. To see the black lizards and the wild goats just feet away from us, then to find ourselves deep in thought about an old man in his monk's tunic drinking rainwater from ancient pots was almost surreal and would have been something we could never have imagined hadn't we seen it for ourselves.

Being in Ibiza for that fortnight with my good friend, Derek Talbot, is a sublime memory from start to finish: From the demonstrations to the spiritual healing, and then falling down that hole and wondering if we'd ever be sober enough to get back to the villa, to climbing that majestic mountain and witnessing a sight that left us emotionally charged with an eeriness of tranquillity. The lovely people we'd made friends with in Ibiza gave us a fabulous send-off, and presented me with several souvenirs, including wine, so much of it that I had to arrange for extra luggage. Our journey back to the UK was lost in thoughts of pleasant exhaustion, with the reward of a good old British pint to look forward to!

My respect for Derek grew exponentially over the years and we remain close friends to this day. A wholly talented sportsman, Derek Talbot MBE achieved an Olympic gold medal, four Commonwealth golds, three European golds, one world singles gold, three All-England golds, eleven national golds, twenty international golds, and eighty-three caps for England. Quite a list, don't you think? And I have had the pleasure and the honour of being his friend for many years.

High-Society Friendships

It would be remiss of me not to mention my very humble and particularly memorable encounter with Diana, Princess of Wales, because it was one of the most honourable times of my life. What a beautiful woman, both inside and out. Her warmth and compassion spoke volumes, and even though she couldn't help but exude sophistication, grace and elegance, she came across as a down-to-earth woman who would do anything to make a person happy, which is exactly what she did do on many occasions. I include myself there, as we shook hands and her smile radiated into my soul. I was introduced to Diana at the very prestigious venue known as Hale Clinic, which was then owned by Teresa Hale. In June 1988, Diana officially opened the clinic, which was situated in Regents Park, London, and it was a few years later, in 1991, when she attended the clinic for treatment, that I was privileged to make her acquaintance.

My meeting with Diana reached the masses and I was subsequently approached by a few journalists asking for an exclusive for their newspapers. For me to have spoken to them about my time with her would have degraded the encounter we had, and she was far too loved by the public for anyone to have done that. To reveal what we talked about or indeed why she attended the clinic, was abhorrent and something I was absolutely loathed to do. And so, I turned them down, much to their disappointment, and watched as each one scurried off with their tail between their legs and their notebooks still empty. I did report their invasion of privacy – for that's how it felt at the time – to Teresa Hale, and never heard anymore about it.

~ ❖ ~

Another famous personality I met through my healing was professional footballer, Ray Kennedy, who played for both Arsenal and Liverpool from the late 1960s to the 1980s. Ray came to me when I practiced in Newcastle, turning up for a healing session donning a fabulous suntan! I didn't know who he was at first, never realised that he was such a brilliant footballer who'd helped Arsenal become the dominant club of English football between 1975 and 1982. They won the division five times, the FA cup four times, the European cup three times, and went on to win the UEFA cup and League cups. He was a true gentleman whom I got to know pretty well, and I classed him as another true friend that I came to admire for many reasons, not least because of his success as a sportsman.

Ray entered my treatment room and I started to work on him, getting him to relax in the hope I would be able to take out the stresses his training would have had on his limbs. "I can't move my feet," he said suddenly, "they're stuck to the floor." I told him not to worry about it as it was just part of the treatment I was giving. He wasn't overly convinced, I could tell when I noticed his puzzled expression, but we got through it, and he was happy to come back. Unfortunately, Ray developed Parkinson's Disease, but I am proud to have those memories and to call him my friend. He was described by football manager, Bob Paisley, as *"One of Liverpool's greatest players, and probably the most underrated."*

~ ❖ ~

I was still travelling up and down the country on a regular basis in those days, as well as travelling to Spain, and on one of my journeys I came across a professional boxer called Glenn McCrory, a six-foot-four cruiser and heavyweight who'd won various titles in his career and lived up to his nickname of 'Gentleman'.

Ian "The Machine" Freeman was another fighter I got to know; he was a cage fighter and a very talented man, and we met at a psychic fair. The thing with Ian was that he was huge, and quite simply a man you didn't mess with. I remember looking him straight in the eye at that fair, having no idea who he was at the time. When he called me over, it took all my strength to keep upright as my legs started to resemble something pretty similar to a dancing jelly! I thought that was it for me, he'd give me one punch and I'd be a goner.

But it was quite the opposite as he suddenly gave me a wide grin and said, "No one has ever looked me straight in the eye before like you just did. You and me are friends." I managed to compose myself and gave this former bouncer from Sunderland a nervous smile back, wondering whether I should shake his hand, pat him on the back, or slowly back away. But like Glenn, he turned out to be a true gentleman and a good friend, and yet another famous personality I was honoured to class as *my* friend. I've attended many of Ian's fights over the years, some at the NEC Birmingham, where he fought Paul Kahoon and beat him hands down. He also put on a lot of fights at the Leisure Centre in Newcastle and the turnout was always massive. Ian would often insist I joined his family at the fights as I'd usually turn up on my own. His kindness also stretched to wavering the fee of my admission! He was tough in the ring and out of it, and could always handle himself no matter what, or indeed who, he was faced with. He went on to become Cage Rage British World Heavyweight Champion and was the first British person to fight in the UFC (Ultimate Fighting Championship), a subsidiary of the Mixed Martial Arts, where he beat American MMA fighter, Frank Mir.

He might be a gentleman, but, like I said, you simply didn't mess with him. He's no pushover, even if he does come across as warm and charming.

Commendably, Ian raised a lot of money for people who needed to pay for private treatment and subsequently gave an awful lot to charities, including the proceeds from a film he made called, *Sucker Punch*, which went to a young man with a rare form of cancer. It's such a privilege for me to know these amazing people, and that's why I wanted to give them all a mention in this book. When it was suggested to me by Dudley Films owner, Peter Cook, to write a book, I agreed. "It'll be fascinating," he said, with genuine feeling. All these people *are* fascinating as they've helped me on this phenomenal journey through my life and continue to do so to this day.

Here are a few short extracts from Ian's biography:

Ian Freeman was born in Sunderland in 1966 and lived an ordinary life until an accident changed its course… A doorman boxer and street fighter, he was the first British fighter ever to enter the notorious Octagon in America's ultimate fighting championship… The first Brit to go over there and win the fight… Ian "The Machine" is recognised as one of the toughest London Godfathers… Show respect and admiration… Has one of the hardest punches…

To Find A Cure

I bumped into Millie Blenkinsop, a close friend of mine, whilst in town one day, and she told me she would be going into hospital soon to have an operation to fix the hole in her bladder. As you'll know by now, I'm not the kind of person who can sit back and watch a friend suffer with pain and so once again, I extended the hand of friendship to this lady and invited her to my clinic. It's always rewarding when someone has faith in me and trusts me to try and help them, and I was glad when Millie took me up on my offer and made herself comfortable on the treatment table. I explained what would happen and put some music on for her to listen to, which would hopefully assist her to relax. Fortunately, it did, and she left that day saying she felt a tingling sensation running down her arms and the backs of her legs: "*A lovely warm feeling,*" she described it as.

Later that same day, Millie checked herself into the hospital where she was to undergo surgery the following morning. Her husband, Graham, was with her, and even though she naturally felt nervous about what would happen, she was also more relaxed than she might have been if she hadn't been to see me earlier on in the day.

After the operation, her surgeon went to see her once she'd come round from the anaesthetic and told her that when it came to carrying out the procedure, there was nothing to operate on because her bladder had healed over. To this day, Millie swears blind that the healing I performed on her had been the cure. She's a very down to earth person and not at all one to sensationalise or exaggerate anything. I was happy enough that she'd just attended my clinic for healing, but the fact that the treatment I gave and her complete faith in what I'd done had been sufficient enough to prevent her needing surgery was a massive boost back then. Millie and I became even closer friends after that and she's another incredible person I am truly honoured to have in my life.

We've known each other thirty-six years now; she's beaten cancer twice and I'm in awe at her strength to carry on. She's always fought every step of the way and has encouraged people the world over to never give up. I've always admired how she tells others they're never too old to learn new things in life, and I can honestly say, hand on heart, that she is an inspiration to all those whom she comes into contact with.

She even brought her Jack Russell dog, Patch, to see me once, after he'd been knocked down by a car. The vet had told her that he'd need operating on to fix his broken pelvis, and even more concerning, that his leg would have to be removed. As you can imagine, Millie was distraught, and when I told her about my successes with animals over the years, she brought him in for healing. I carefully lifted him onto the table and got to work on him. The poor little thing was shaking and nervous, and most likely in considerable pain. He looked up at me a few times as I was treating him, his brown eyes pleading as though to say, "*Help me*," and I was determined to at least make him comfortable.

The next day, Millie rang me to say Patch seemed to be back to his old self, but she would still take him to the vet later in the day. The news was positive, and the vet confirmed that his leg was absolutely fine. I'll never forgot those eyes boring into mine on that table for as long as I live, and I was thrilled that I'd given that lovely little dog another chance to chase a ball and beg for treats.

Family Values

The spiritual healing had become a huge part of my life and I decided it was time to move into other fields of a spiritual nature as well. And so, after thinking about the areas I wanted to develop my skills into next, I discovered a significant interest in hypnotherapy. I managed to get four diplomas in this field and practiced for some time, whilst still continuing my healing practices. This area of expertise took me to psychic fairs along with Mind, Body and Spirit events and I then started to undergo a lot more with clairvoyance and mediumship. The work built up and I got myself known in these circles too, mainly through word of mouth, which I've always found is the best way to develop your associates.

I got to know many good people, and one family in particular that I remember with fondness was the Dhanda's, some lovely people who I'd like to give a mention to. They contacted me in the hope I could help their father who had cancer. Even though he was responding well to his medical treatment, the family asked if I could help out by perhaps speeding up his recovery progress. I was honoured to assist and began to administer spiritual healing to Mr Dhanda on several occasions until he finally went into remission, and I'm pleased to say that he lived for many years after he'd fully recovered. I do believe his recovery was aided by a combination of both my healing and the medical treatment he received, and I got to know his family quite well over time. I'd fly from Newcastle to Heathrow to visit where they lived in London and subsequently became good friends with Mr Dhanda's son, Paul.

On one weekend visit, Paul showed me around London, including the temple he and his family attended, and introduced me to his fascinating world of Indian culture. I found it incredibly enlightening and was honoured to have been invited to learn about religious beliefs quite different to our own. I recall Paul's mum and how kind she was when she bought me some shirts from Oxford Street, making me feel a true part of their family. She unfortunately passed away from cancer, and although peacefully, it was still very sad at the time. A lovely, warm and gentle lady with strong family values and a beautiful mind. I've stayed friendly with the Dhanda family to this day and still get invites to their home.

Convincing A Sceptic

I was starting to get well-known in the world of clairvoyance by now and had built up a large audience of people who would follow me from show to show as I picked them out and delivered a much-needed message from a passed loved one. Everyone who attends a show hopes a message will come through for them and even though there might be a few sceptics in the audience, the majority are elated when I point to them and single them out, then tell them the message that's being conveyed to me. It's another rewarding moment when I know someone might have been desperate to hear from a loved one they still mourn, and it happens, in front of many other people, all sitting in awe at the thought of their belief in life-after-death coming true.

A friend of mine, Stan Sinclair, never used to believe in the afterlife, and in the fifty-eight years we've known each other, we've had our ups and downs and discussions about it. He always believed that once you're dead, you've gone. That's the end. No coming back. It was a continuing difference of opinion between us, and I would sometimes have to agree to disagree for want of not falling out with him. But one time, he agreed to take part in a demonstration I'd been asked to perform for a newspaper article. It was during a weekend in Cumbria and having set up the stage, people started to arrive to watch, and Stan, still unable to bring himself to believe, got ready with me as the journalist sat poised with his pen and notebook.

Stan had a bad back in those days and I suggested doing some spiritual healing on him in front of our audience. He'd received an injury during his time in the army and had lived with the pain for quite some time. When I started to work on him, with the audience in silence and the only sound heard being the journalist's pen frantically scribbling across the paper of his notebook, Stan suddenly asked me, "Where's that heat coming from?" It was flowing through the affected area of his back and obviously making a difference to the constant pain he was in. He even admitted the healing I'd performed had given him relief and from then on, he decided to take more of an interest in my work.

Did he really believe after that? I'm honestly not sure. But he did assist me on the odd occasions when I performed live shows, so perhaps he became a lot more open-minded about the whole thing. I wasn't trying to convince him there is life after death as that was something only he could decide for himself, but he watched me continue to treat people and perform on stage in front of an audience, and I was more than happy to know that he wasn't quite so cynical anymore.

Psychic Fairs

My good friend, Tina, encouraged me to pass my driving test. I'd failed the first time, but in 1995 I took it again, and with Tina's support, I'm pleased to say I passed! We did, however, drift apart when I got really busy with workshops and talk shows, but we always remained friends. If it hadn't been for Tina, I'm not sure I'd have got through it the second time either, but after I finally got my licence, it gave me much more freedom and independence to drive around the country to attend psychic fairs and courses, and I'll forever be grateful to her for being there, pushing me in the right direction, probably knowing it would lead to a whole new venture.

My very first psychic fair was at The Queen's Arms in Bishop Auckland. I hadn't got a clue what to expect or what I'd be expected to do, or even how I was supposed to decorate my allotted table with paraphernalia. When I arrived, I was shown to my stall, situated next to a nice guy who introduced himself to me as Ray White. Ray kindly lent me a tablecloth and showed me how to display my items to potential passing clients, and helped me get myself sorted, explaining the procedure and the structure of what was usually done at one of these events. He was a great tarot card reader and very popular with the people who attended. He was also a wealth of knowledge and during the course of the fair, he introduced me to some of the people he knew and told me about other psychic fairs around the country. I was hugely grateful to him of course and found myself attending many fairs after that – Edinburgh, Glasgow, Dundee, and Aberdeen throughout Scotland, and Yorkshire, Hampshire, Berkshire, and London in England, to name just a few places I visited.

I was thrilled to get fully booked up with clients at each fair and started to travel around with a couple of friends, Trudy Ashpland and Mary Holcroft. The ladies would book hotels and accommodation for us all and we'd all go there together, doing Mind, Body and Spirit events in different parts of the country. This went on every weekend, and I was meeting some wonderful people from all walks of life.

During the week, I'd get together with some of the people I'd met at these events, and we would book pubs, community halls and hotels to perform short demonstrations in front of an audience, which would then be followed by private readings. Coming together like this was a great way for us all to get out there and get ourselves known, and it was also fabulously sociable as we got to know each other. Wherever we went, we always had a good laugh and some great banter. We might have been exhausted afterwards, but it was so worth it.

I was pretty nervous when the time came that I was asked to get on the 'big' stage, the place where the more well-known mediums and psychics would perform, and it was quite overwhelming to see the massive audience all awaiting my direction. I was grateful to a fellow medium called Sean, whom I classed as a lot more confident than me at that time, and definitely more experienced as a performing medium, but his kindness often made me feel at ease and he'd tell me: "*We all work differently; none of us are the same.*"

As time went by and my confidence began to build, I was invited to take the floor at Spiritualist churches, which, even though was often a trial-and-error exercise not knowing if anything would happen, it was also a massive reward when something *did* happen and I was able to help someone find closure. I got huge satisfaction from those events in seeing someone's eyes light up or a nod of the head, or just a simple "*thanks*" that would be whispered through tears and relief.

One lady I did a reading for had lost her husband, Mick, and was thrilled, if not surprised, when I managed to connect with him. Brenda Stokoe lived in Sunderland and it was evident that she missed him terribly. Hearing me tell her he was now safe and no longer in pain, along with the fact he was looking out for her brought her great comfort and it was once again a pleasure to be able to communicate a message to someone to whom those few words meant the world. It was through Brenda that I met Mick's father, David, a great guy and a very well-known and respected man in Sunderland and the surrounding areas. When I met him, he didn't believe in the spirit world and kept asking me endless questions about what I did, how it happened, *what* would happen, as though he was fascinated to know and learn.

David had a bit of a reputation – he still has – but if you're lucky enough to get to know him, you'll most definitely agree with me that he's a true gentleman and a very hard-working man. His family are good people, and I include his brother, Lee, in that statement. The thing with David was that I could see something special about him and told him he had the ability to be clairvoyant. Odd things happened to him over the years and other psychics had told him the same thing. I do think that perhaps as he gets older, he may take his psychic abilities further and develop more.

Letters, Extracts & Testimonies

I've always received lots of letters since starting my work from people I've helped either with healing or clairvoyance, or by doing readings for when they want to tell me about certain things that they later discovered were accurate and true. They perhaps couldn't confirm my accuracy during the actual reading and often couldn't wait to get home and ask a relative. But knowing that people want to keep in touch has always been a great compliment to me, and one lady called Jude Eltringham wrote to me once in connection with a show I did for her to raise money for a charity in Berwick-upon-Tweed in Northumberland:

Dear Noel

I don't suppose that you remember me, but you kindly did an evening of clairvoyance for me to raise funds. I remember that you said during the performance that some of your messages would be ignored during the live part of the show, but that people would comment on your accuracy in the interval.

Well, two people there that night were related to one of the girls from the Worlds End murders in Edinburgh. They were shocked by your accuracy and until the court case, had no idea that someone they knew for many years, who was present, gave evidence that he was a former boyfriend of the same girl.

This was just one letter that verified my communication with the spirit world to be true. The letters poured in, from all walks of life and from all over the country, including some from abroad, and that made me feel extremely humble. I knew the messages I was giving needed to be heard - spirit would never make contact with me through these events for no reason - and when these people acknowledged that communication, giving me feedback as well, it just made for a much more worthwhile experience all round.

Testimony received from Ann Brown:

I made an appointment to see Noel and I felt very apprehensive about it. I was suffering with anxiety and withdrawals and almost did not want to go to my first session. However, that first meeting with Noel dispelled my doubts.

Noel explained his work and procedures in an open and friendly way, which I was able to relate to and understand straight away. He was happy to answer questions and was honest in his explanations of what he could do.

I was diagnosed in late July 1989 with cervical cancer at an inoperable stage. The only treatment they could offer me then was radiotherapy with only a 50-60% success rate over a five-year period of time. They couldn't begin the treatment for two months.

I saw Noel's spiritual healing work affect my life from three separate viewpoints: My physical health, mental health, and spiritual well-being. Throughout the treatment, Noel was able to tell me, with confidence, that the cancer was receding. The actual sessions allowed me to have the mental energy to retain a positive attitude and strengthen my religious beliefs.

In January the following year, my doctors confirmed Noel's view that healing had indeed taken place both physically and spiritually.

Testimony received from Mrs D Cook, Garston, Watford:

31ˢᵗ August 1990

I first consulted Mr Sorbie in July. I suffered severe pain in my legs due to arthritis and was finding it increasingly difficult to stand for any length of time. I was having terrible trouble walking, getting out of a chair, and even getting out of bed, and had great difficulty climbing the stairs. I was constantly taking pain killers in the hope to gain a little relief from my discomfort.

I could not wear ladies' shoes and instead had to wear men's. I always had to rely on a walking stick to get around, and my life became an utter misery.

I consulted with Mr Sorbie six times over the last few months and can honestly say I feel like a different person. I have to admit that I was somewhat sceptical at first and incredibly nervous on my first visit. But he made me feel very relaxed and very confident, and I am so happy I went to seek his help.

This following extract is taken from an article in 'Soul and Spirit' Magazine:

Tales of the Unexplained: Liz Alvis Investigates Linda Smith, 42, from Hornchurch - "I had a terrifying brush with a shadowy figure"

"I used to work as a cleaner in a warehouse. One day, while going about my work, I felt something strange, as though someone were stood right behind me. When I turned around, the sight that greeted me was one I'll never forget: A shadowy figure was standing there, now in front of me. I couldn't make out its features, but I sensed it was more masculine in shape than feminine. I turned away again not knowing what to do or say, but when I looked back, the figure had gone."

I asked Noel what Linda may have experienced, and his explanation was that he felt she had encountered her Guardian Angel looking out for her. He said there was no need to feel afraid but to feel comforted by its presence.

An extract from a lady called Gemma described how she felt something bad was going to happen, and when I tuned into her energy, I told her she had received a warning of some kind. I wasn't going to tell her what that warning entailed, but unfortunately, six months later, her good friend passed away suddenly.

Another humble moment for me came after doing a reading for a young lady known as Duffy Jones, a singer who became famous in the early 2000s. Duffy had been referred to me by a friend of hers from London. It was a phone reading and even though at the time I had no idea who she was, I was able to describe her appearance over the phone and confirm that I knew her real name was actually Aimee and that she was Welsh. From that we built a connection, and I was able to give her a detailed reading for which she was extremely grateful. When she asked how much I charged, I told her I would be happy with a donation, which is something I rarely do. A few days later I received a cheque in the post for £120, signed personally by 'Duffy Jones'. It was a particularly generous donation that was also accompanied by a personal note:

Hello Noel

It was lovely to have spoken to you. Thank you so much for your time. We will definitely keep in contact.

Love, Duffy.

I gave her a follow-up reading sometime later and this time she sent me another donation of £150, so you can appreciate why I felt so humble. This beautiful woman with a stunning singing voice, very much in the public eye back then, was down-to-earth and possessed a lovely, warm heart. It was an honour to know her and be able to read for her. Sadly, I lost touch with her after the second reading as a lot was going on in both our lives, but she touched my heart with her generosity and personal warmth.

LETTERS, EXTRACTS & TESTIMONIES

Epilogue

You've now read a lot about my life and about how I've thrown myself into my work. I've had a wealth of experience since being born and it's all led me to where I am today. I can look back on some of my time with fondness, whilst thinking back on some of it with a tinge of sadness. But however we live our lives, whatever journey we embark upon, it is a map laid out for our higher self to work through, allowing it to make the right choices and fall back into line when we make the wrong ones.

Everyone's life is an experience. As individuals, no experience can be exactly the same, and we all find different paths along the way in which to tread and explore our surroundings. Some may unintentionally cause harm or hurt to others simply because it's a way to learn and know our boundaries as we grow. Our souls are tested as challenges lie ahead, and some of those challenges are not always the easy option. As we mature, we are able to judge for ourselves how difficult or easy that challenge will be, and many people will often choose the easy route. We can become fearful or uncomfortable about something, which might then lead us to make the decision that we'd rather not pursue what we deem to be the unknown.

People who do not wish to learn about their inner life can continue to live of their own free-will; this is just a choice that we, as human beings, are entitled to make. However, when people choose to live a spiritual path like I have done, it gives us the encouragement and the determination to listen, learn, and appreciate that our higher self has something to say. It maybe that our experiences are in harmony with the needs of the soul and following a spiritual path will give us the opportunity to connect on a higher level.

In addition to our learning, we need a considerable amount of courage to do what our higher self suggests and if we are unable to find that courage, the fear will set in and cause our free-will to vary our actions. Willpower and dedication are paramount when following the spiritual path, and this is something I have learnt myself over the decades.

When we choose to listen to our higher self, we are tested to overcome our fears.

As I've talked about in this book, there are beings far wiser than we are who help us to understand the true journey we embark upon. These beings are known as Guardian Angels or Guides, and they stay by our sides to protect and keep us safe, ensuring our own journey follows the path it was destined to tread. Every individual veers off that path, of course, but our Angels encourage us back.

Throughout our lives, these Guides will change. We are always learning and experiencing changes, either in a personal capacity or in our working life. Our spiritual path moves onto many different levels and at each one, as we move up to a higher plane of existence, these Guides will step back and allow another to take their place. As explained in the Introduction, we also call these Angels or Guides, 'Doorkeepers', which gives you an insight into how your life will unfold as you go through another door on this journey.

"*As one door closes, another one opens...*" And by each door is a new keeper to guide you further along your spiritual path.

None of us will ever experience only the good in our lives. That would be unrealistic and quite unbelievable. Even though I have always known I've been protected from being a young boy, I've lived through some truly horrendous times, some of which I've mentioned in this book. My experience with Trisha was unforgettably sad, as were other incidences where I've lost loved ones or had to say goodbye. These are all events that can, and often do happen to us, and which help us to grow and realise the circle of life is such a precious one. I knew I didn't need to be afraid deep down, but it never stopped me, because that's an inevitable human reaction. Something might happen to us that we don't expect, and it can lead to us spiralling out of control, leaving us feeling dejected and lost and unable to comprehend what this life really is about.

Throughout my journey, I once found myself homeless and living on the streets in London, and in order to be able to afford the simplest meal, I became a busker in Euston Station, relying on people throwing their pocket change into my hat so that I could at least treat myself to a cup of coffee and perhaps a sandwich. I sometimes saw the bad in people in those days as they looked at me with utter contempt, their eyes suggesting that I was the lowest of the low for having no home and being a beggar on a street. They were just going about their business, carrying on with their lives, probably hoping to get from A to B without too much fuss. Yet I was also going about *my* life, trying to make a little money to eat and drink and perhaps get myself back on my feet again. Both them and I were simply trying to make ends meet – even though our lives were so far apart, we still had something in common.

Since those days, I learnt how quickly life can suddenly take a turn for the worse; how people can find themselves with constant hot running water and a bag of groceries one day, then having to rely on public toilets and spare change from a kind passer-by the next. I have the utmost respect for those people. Not all of them are homeless through choice. Many are simply going through a difficult time in their lives and often find that their own journey needs to be veered back to where it should be. They may not have chosen the spiritual path like I did, but in turn, they don't deserve to be homeless or living a life of uncertainty.

As my own life was steered back in the right direction and I continued to follow my calling, I knew that by helping others in the way I was able to, be it healing, hypnotism, clairvoyance, mediumship, or by simply being a good friend, that was what *my* life was about. It is the best feeling in the world to know you've helped someone - don't you agree? It's pretty amazing to watch the recognition on someone's face, either in an audience or during a one-to-one reading, and know they are on your level when they smile, or cry, and confirm their belief in what you're relaying to them. Messages and guidance from those who still protect us from their own spiritual journey are the most credible affirmation we need and can often help us to live again in the knowledge that our loved ones are around us. They don't feel pain or heartache in the spirit world, but they may feel yours on the earth plane, and all they ask is that you be happy and carry on your own life's journey knowing a little bit more about your higher self.

My next book, available in 2022, will contain readings and messages from the spirit world, given to those who have sought my help. And whilst some of the stories I have will fascinate you, others will make you smile, some might make you laugh, and some

could even make you cry as I give you an insight into how my life has materialised so eclectically over the years. I look forward to regaling you once again with the wonderful people who grace my life, whether they reside on our earth plane or in the spirit world.

I hope you have enjoyed my debut book and found a little peace and enlightenment as you've read about the story of my life so far. I would love to hear from you, and I list below a few ways you can make contact:

Facebook: Noel Sorbie, Clairvoyant Medium

https://www.facebook.com/noel.sorbie.31

Email: rbie2@msn.com

Mobile/WhatsApp: (44) 07525 774525

Acknowledgements

First and foremost, my most sincere gratitude will always go to my parents, Frederick and Lilian Charlotte Sorbie, for bringing me into this world and giving me the opportunity to experience all of its wonders, thus enabling me to make a difference to so many people. Their love and support graced me with my dedication to do good, to live a full life and always look forward to what lay ahead. Their encouragement and belief in me was phenomenal and I thank God every day for being blessed to have had these two wonderful people in my life.

Pam Carter also believed in me, and I want to give my thanks to her for always being there, by my side, offering me much-needed love, support, and encouragement when I felt like giving up. Pam got on my case and made me realise how much I needed to get this autobiography out there. She was my rock and I thank her with all my heart.

One person that had huge influence in the writing of this book is my good friend, Derek Talbot MBE. His support and friendship have been an inspiration in the making of this autobiography, and I'll be forever grateful to him.

I wish to give a mention, along with my humble thanks, to Millie Blenkinsop for her devoted friendship and support, along with her son, James Bulman. Rest in Peace.

Huge thanks go to Richard Howden, Photographer, who took the photographs for the book cover. And along with Richard, I wish to say thank you to Hammad Khalid, Graphic Designer, who created the book cover from the photographs and went to great lengths to format the interior to a professional standard.

Peter Cook, Producer & Director of Dudley Films, deserves my thanks also, for inspiring me many years ago to put pen to paper and write this book about my life's journey.

Last, but not least, my thanks go to Kathryn Hall, Author & Editor, for her support, professionalism, and excellent writing, putting this book together which also included research. Kathryn is a genuine friend who has helped me every way she can to accomplish my dream. I reached out to the universe and there she was: I thank God for that day!

There are many people I could mention in this section because I've met so many throughout my life, so thank you to all my friends from all over the world for being there for me and believing in me.

A mention also to Brett Treacy and Maggie Shannon, both incredible healers from Australia.

Printed in Great Britain
by Amazon